Informal Learning
and
FIELD TRIPS

Informal Learning and FIELD TRIPS

Engaging Students in Standards-Based Experiences Across the K–5 Curriculum

Leah M. Melber   Foreword by Doris B. Ash

CORWIN PRESS
A SAGE Company
Thousand Oaks, CA 91320

Copyright © 2008 by Corwin Press.

For information:

Corwin Press
A SAGE Company
2455 Teller Road
Thousand Oaks, California 91320
www.corwinpress.com

SAGE Ltd.
1 Oliver's Yard
55 City Road
London EC1Y 1SP
United Kingdom

SAGE India Pvt. Ltd.
B 1/I 1 Mohan Cooperative Industrial Area
Mathura Road, New Delhi 110 044
India

SAGE Asia-Pacific Pte. Ltd.
33 Pekin Street #02–01
Far East Square
Singapore 048763

Printed in the United States of America

Library of Congress Cataloging-in-Publication Data

Melber, Leah M.
Informal learning and field trips: engaging students in standards-based experiences across the K–5 curriculum / Leah M. Melber.
    p. cm.
Includes bibliographical references and index.
ISBN 978-1-4129-4979-8 (cloth)
ISBN 978-1-4129-4980-4 (pbk.)
    1. School field trips. 2. Education, Elementary—Activity programs. 3. Education—Standards. I. Title.

LB1047.M425 2008
372.13′8—dc22   2007019368

This book is printed on acid-free paper.

07   08   09   10   11   10   9   8   7   6   5   4   3   2   1

Acquisitions Editor:	Cathy Hernandez
Editorial Assistant:	Megan Bedell
Production Editor:	Libby Larson
Copy Editor:	Glenn Wright
Typesetter:	C & M Digitals (P) Ltd.,
Proofreader:	Theresa Kay
Indexer:	Michael Ferreira
Cover Designer:	Michael Dubowe
Graphic Designer:	Karine Hovsepian

Contents

Foreword

*I*nformal Learning and Field Trips: Engaging Students in Standards-Based Experiences Across the K–5 Curriculum *is the book we have been waiting for. By we, I mean the teachers, researchers, and docents working with learners in classrooms, museums, aquariums, zoos, and other places of learning. This is a time of extraordinary interest in out-of-school learning and teaching. Research, texts, and pedagogies, however, have not yet caught up with such heightened interest. We have been hungry for expertise that crosses from classroom to museums and back again.

Informal Learning and Field Trips makes such essential connections for teachers who want to make full use of their community's resources. In these days of standardized testing, paperwork, and special needs, teachers want, need, and deserve to have their out-of-school, field trip time facilitated, so that they can spend quality time teaching their students rather than worrying about logistics. This text is aimed at teachers seeking information about how to maximize their efforts as well as how to best serve their students.

Informal Learning and Field Trips also begins to take down the walls between in-classroom and out-of-classroom teaching and learning, letting us know how to use classrooms, the outdoors, and museums seamlessly. Over the past decade, those geographical locations have been conflated with the kind of learning and teaching that occurs in them. Many of us, however, believe that learning has the same fundamental characteristics whether it takes place at home, in school, or in a museum. Dr. Melber has encouraged docents and teachers alike to crisscross learning landscapes using powerful ideas, specific content, and intentional teaching activities.

As Dr. Melber has worked in both schools and in museums, she is eminently qualified to present such teaching strategies across context and content areas. The five specialized chapters, each matched to particular content areas and national content standards, allow teachers interested in math, science, or art to find meaningful, creative, practical activities. Such a rich selection of materials has heretofore not been available.

Informal Learning and Field Trips is brimming with other valuable resources. Besides the things one might expect, such as Web sites, addresses, information about fees and buses, and other nitty-gritty essentials, Dr. Melber provides vignettes that allow an instant glimpse into a field trip, complete with teacher dialogue, expectations, and how success might look. I have found these vignettes particularly useful. Such vignettes provide one vision of success; the evaluation rubrics provide another. I am especially impressed by Dr. Melber's guidelines for making discussion an essential part of pre-, mid-, and after-trip activities. Such activities are greatly enhanced by the suggested ways to evaluate student participation.

My final comments relate to the tone of *Informal Learning and Field Trips*. This is an intelligent book aimed at intelligent (but busy) teachers. Dr. Melber's activities are easy to understand, yet rich, and most important they span from classroom to field trip in a seamless fashion that connects teaching and learning in all their guises.

—Doris B. Ash

Preface

There was a time when a field trip was considered a "free day," an opportunity to focus on fun and put learning goals aside. It might be a chance to sit next to your best friend on the bus or purchase a special pencil from the gift shop. Over the years, however, the true value of field trips as quality learning experiences has become more apparent to teachers and researchers alike. But it is not enough simply to grow a research base or theoretical support for a field such as *informal learning*, or learning outside the context of a traditional classroom setting. Many professionals have also come to recognize the need for practitioner-based information in support of these quality connections. This book seeks to serve as one resource in meeting this need, providing pragmatic links between the classroom and the surrounding community.

Having spent time both as an elementary classroom teacher and as a museum educator and researcher, I have had the opportunity to approach field trips from many different perspectives. As a museum educator, I have felt significant disappointment when a class comes and goes without taking advantage of unique museum programs or materials. As a classroom teacher, I have been frustrated by admission lines and galleries not well suited to my third-grade students. As an educational researcher, I have seen the impact a well-crafted field trip experience can have on student learning. As a university professor, I have worked with student teachers to identify alternatives to field trips when there simply isn't funding for a bus. This book draws on all of these experiences, taking into account the logistics of classroom expectations while striving for field trip experiences that truly provide a real-world context for learning.

Perhaps most important, this book contains the voices of the many teachers and students I have spoken to over the years: the overall excitement surrounding field trips, a teacher's feelings of confusion when faced with creating a field trip lesson, and the sense of pride on the part of students and teachers over a particularly successful experience. This work also contains the voice of educational researchers who have worked for years to establish a theoretical base to support informal learning as a necessity, not a luxury. All of these professionals I call my colleagues, and many of them I also call friends. Their tireless efforts to document and investigate the process of learning outside the classroom provide the theoretical grounding for this book. Last, this work contains the voice of informal educators themselves, whose mission is simply to share the rich offerings of their respective institutions with the general public and learners of all ages.

A LOOK INSIDE

The work begins with an introductory chapter written to excite the reader with the possibilities that a specially crafted field trip holds. In addition, it explores logistical concerns to assist educators with preparing for a field trip aligned with the policies and regulations of schools and school districts. Chapters 2 through 6 treat each academic area separately, providing suggestions for field trip destinations as well as concrete activities to be implemented during the field trip experience. These lessons are integrated across the curriculum and tied to national standards in order to facilitate their inclusion within an already full curriculum. Assessment suggestions as well as possible extension activities are another critical component of these content chapters.

Chapter 7 provides background on the importance of the field trip experience to students receiving special education services as well as English learners. Chapter 8 specifically addresses the role that technology can play in both enhancing off-site field trips and serving as replacement activities when an off-site visit is not possible. Chapter 9 recognizes the importance of administrative approval, summarizes research, and provides classroom educators with rationales to support off-site excursions. Chapter 10 recognizes that even with such resources, many educators will not be able to take as many field trips as they would like. Thus Chapter 10 provides ideas for alternative activities that, while conducted within a classroom, can incorporate the process skills of field trip investigations. Chapter 11 provides information on the different resources informal learning sites can provide teachers, from professional development opportunities to free curriculum materials. Chapter 12 briefly concludes the work, sharing a third-grade teacher's successful field trip vignette. At this point, the reader is encouraged to put into practice the many ideas from the work.

USING THE CONTENT CHAPTERS

As discussed above, Chapters 2 through 6 are devoted to specific academic areas within the elementary curriculum. These are some of the richest chapters, with a large amount of information to support the reader.

Each of these chapters begins with the latest research in best practices within that academic area and how field trips can best support what's happening in the classroom. These chapters then profile several common field-trip destinations in line with the specific academic discipline. For each location, two model activities are provided. One is intended for use at grade levels K–2 and the other at grade levels 3–5. Sometimes these activities are quite similar to each other, with only minor modifications to take into account different developmental levels. In other cases, they may be quite different. You'll notice that while each activity is tailored to a particular site and academic area of focus, they might utilize similar skills, such as note taking, journal completion, or oral presentation. That's because these skills are the basis for authentic experiences with all subject matter, linked to work of professionals in the field. Each activity is tightly linked to national standards.

For each activity, a suggested evaluation rubric is presented. Some activities are best assessed through a basic credit or no-credit rubric. In this case, specific behaviors or performances that would be expected for a student to earn credit for participation are presented. For those activities with a culminating project or product requiring more detailed assessment, three- and four-point rubric scales are presented. These rubrics can be used to provide each student with an assessment score, or to assign a single score to an entire cooperative group with minor modification from the teacher. Each teacher is encouraged to use an assessment system in line with school procedures, simply using these rubrics as a starting place for evaluating these rich field trip projects.

Also presented in these chapters are several related Web sites for each destination. These Web sites can be helpful in planning a field trip or can serve as a replacement activity when a field trip is not possible. Significant care was taken to select sites connected with institutions and organizations that have an established history and thus are likely to be present in the years to come. However, the Internet is a quickly evolving resource and some sites may change over time.

Although this book is organized with individual chapters provided for each academic area, the activities are all integrated across the curriculum. Museums and other field trip destinations provide excellent opportunities for projects integrated across several curricular areas. A science investigation at a zoo is likely to depend on skilled note taking and computation. A mathematical exploration of a local cemetery will have clear ties to social science investigations. While including these activities within the classroom curriculum, it's likely you'll be able to meet a number of standards beyond those listed within the subject-specific chapters. Each of these activities can be easily modified to add greater emphasis to a particular academic area, in line with your own classroom goals.

With thousands of field trip destinations and as many or more activity possibilities, it would be impossible for any one volume to serve as an exhaustive resource. Rather, this work seeks to spark new discussion on how the classroom curriculum and field trip destinations can work together to support the needs of all elementary learners.

It's now time for some serious field trip planning. Let's begin.

ACKNOWLEDGMENTS

I am eternally grateful for the assistance and support I received during the creation of this book. I'd like to first thank those who generously provided specific chapter assistance and advice: Elizabeth Smith, special education teacher extraordinaire; Stephanie Pryor, artist as well as art teacher; Sarah Marcotte and her ever-growing knowledge of the connections between informal learning and technological advances; and Josh Niklason, Monica Kohlblatz, and Colleen Kessler for their willingness to share their personal stories.

A thank-you to my university colleagues for their overarching support of the project: Dr. Kimberly Persiani-Becker, with her confidence in my concept and patience in explaining the tedious process of publication; Dr. Amy Cox-Petersen as my research partner over the years, with whom I explored so many ways to connect classroom instruction and museum visits; my fellow researchers worldwide who work in the informal sector, and whose prior research supports the direction we are all moving today; Dr. Doris Ash for her willingness to author the book's foreword in the midst of a demanding schedule; and Dr. Robert Rueda for his support in making connections between the field of informal learning and the broader education community.

I would like to thank the many classroom teachers—too numerous to count—who have touched this work, through either a personal story of field trip success or an offhand lament of what could have gone better. They are the inspiration for creating a work that is as pragmatic as it is far reaching. A special thank-you to Conchi Brown for highlighting the importance of order, Julie Beckman for reminding us of the need for creative chaos, and my CSULA students as exemplars of the hundreds of new teachers that join the ranks each academic year, eager to take that first field trip and for any guidance in making that trip a successful one.

I would also like to thank my former colleagues at "The Museum." My experiences there were guiding influences in the development of this work, especially the desire to create a "touchdown" museum experience for students and teachers, as well as knowing when to punt. Last, a special thank-you goes to Carol Ragan for being the first person generously to invite me into the field of informal education so many years ago. Thank you, Carol, I've decided to stay.

Publisher's Acknowledgments

Corwin Press gratefully acknowledges the contributions of the following reviewers:

Donna Adkins, Kindergarten Teacher
Louisa E. Perritt Primary School, Arkadelphia, AR

Christine Brothers, High-School Science Department Chair
Falmouth High School, Falmouth, MA

Tom Chenoweth, Professor of Educational Policy, Foundations, and
  Administrative Studies
Portland State University, Portland, OR

Amy Cox-Peterson, Associate Professor of Elementary and
  Bilingual Education
California State University, Fullerton, CA

Annette Dake, Elementary Teacher for the Gifted
Bridge Creek Elementary School, Blanchard, OK

Jennifer Harper, Fourth-Grade Teacher
Cavendish Town Elementary School, Proctorsville, VT

Mark Johnson, Principal and Curriculum and Assessment Facilitator
Glenwood Elementary School, Kearney, NE

Linda Jones, Associate Professor of Science and Environmental Education
University of Florida, Gainesville, FL

Pender Kimball, School Director
REAL School, Windham, ME

Nancy Krenner, Fifth-Grade Teacher
Red Rock Elementary School, Woodbury, MN

Alexis Ludewig, Resource Teacher
Saint Germain Elementary School, Saint Germain, WI

Michael Marlow, Associate Professor of Science Education
University of Colorado, Denver, CO

Lauren Mitterman, Middle-School English and Social Studies Teacher
Gibraltar Middle School, Fish Creek, WI

Rob Mocarsky, Kindergarten Teacher
Forest Hills School, Jackman, ME

Debi Molina-Walters, Clinical Assistant Professor
Arizona State University, Polytechnic campus, Mesa, AZ

Pamela Opel, Fifth-Grade Teacher
Pass Road Elementary School, Gulfport, MS

Barbara Rudiak, Executive Director of K–5 Schools
Pittsburgh Public Schools, Pittsburgh, PA

Robert Rueda, Professor of Education
University of Southern California, Los Angeles, CA

Kael Sagheer, Former Elementary-School Teacher
Willa Cather Elementary School, Omaha, NE

Elizabeth Senger, Associate Professor of Education
Auburn University, Auburn, AL

About the Author

 **Leah M. Melber**, PhD, has over fifteen years of experience within the formal and informal education sector. She has served on teams supporting the creation of exhibits, developed several professional development programs aimed at connecting classroom teachers with museum resources, and authored curriculum to better bridge classroom and informal learning experiences. Dr. Melber holds a BA in zoology, an MA in education together with a multiple-subject teaching certification in the state of California, and a PhD in educational psychology from the University of Southern California. She has over twenty refereed publications exploring the dynamics of informal and formal education and how they can best intersect. She is currently an assistant professor in the Charter College of Education at California State University, Los Angeles.

Where to Begin?

Planning for Field Trips

Can you remember your first field trip? It's likely that you do! Though research shows elementary-school field trips are remembered well into adulthood, many times those memories are not completely connected to the actual content or emotional goals of the visit (Falk & Dierking, 1997). We may remember riding a bus with our friends, a unique object on display, or a marble staircase. Maybe we can recall exactly what we ate that day and what exhibit we visited first. Maybe it is just a vague feeling of going on a special adventure that day. With the knowledge that field trips are memorable even decades later, the importance of structuring field trip experiences in a manner that can best support both cognitive and emotional or affective gains becomes clear.

MORE THAN MUSEUMS

When we think of a field trip, it's possible that the local museum or zoo may be the first destinations to come to mind. However, field trips are much more than museums. Researchers may struggle with a single definition for informal learning experiences but generally agree that they encompass unique experiences outside a traditional classroom setting. This may include visits to the beach or a presentation from a park ranger. It includes a visit to an art museum but also a trip to a local gallery with the chance to paint alongside an artist. These informal learning experiences offer a unique chance for students to connect with the world around them and require a slightly different approach to instruction in order to fully tap into their offerings.

Research has shown that both teachers and museum educators may sometimes structure informal learning experiences as they would a classroom environment (Cox-Petersen, Marsh, Kisiel, & Melber, 2003; Seedfeldt, 2005; Taylor, Morris, & Cordeau-Young, 1997). However, researchers recommend that these experiences be structured with an emphasis on student choice, intrinsic motivation, and active investigation (e.g., Csikszentmihalyi & Hermanson, 1995; Wolins, Jensen, & Ulzheimer, 1992). With a to-do list a mile long, and not enough hours in the day, many educators may simply not have the time to prioritize creating a special activity for a one-day field trip. This book hopes to lend busy teachers a helping hand in putting together truly special field trip experiences.

SELECTING THE RIGHT LOCATION

Selecting an appropriate field trip site is the first step to a successful experience. With hundreds of accredited zoos and aquariums and thousands of museums in the United States, selecting between these traditional field trip destinations can be very difficult. When our traditional definition of field trips is expanded to include libraries, parks, retail stores, or historical monuments, the possibilities become endless. The following guidelines may help with selection of an appropriate field trip site for your students and the classroom curriculum.

1. **Curricular Connection:** This is perhaps the most important consideration in designing a successful field trip. In order to provide the maximum benefit, field trips should be established as a critical reinforcement component of the classroom curriculum. A local history museum is a perfect match for students studying Native American cultures. The zoo connects well to classroom studies of adaptations. Some locations, such as a local library, can be connected with almost any curricular area.

2. **Travel Requirements:** For a field trip to have the greatest impact on students, you'll want to have enough time for quality exploration of the site. If students will spend more time on the bus getting to and returning from the site than at the location itself, you may want to rethink your destination. Being rushed through a field trip experience can be more detrimental than not going at all.

3. **Developmental Appropriateness:** Educators are well aware of the different developmental levels students go through as they age. When selecting a field trip site, it is important to select a location that will best match students' developmental level. In addition to content, the method of interpretation should be also considered. Informal learning sites vary in their exhibition style as well as the amount of funding to keep exhibits updated and relevant to diverse audiences. Younger students might be frustrated with a field trip experience focused mainly on text above their reading level and minimal interaction with objects, specimens, or other visuals. It is important to check that the selected destination is aligned with teacher expectations and students' agenda.

LOGISTICS

While the focus of this book is primarily on creating and conducting quality learning activities and projects, all good visits will start with logistical planning. The following checklist addresses some basic considerations to ensure the health and safety of students during an off-campus trip.

Before the trip . . .

- Visit the intended field trip site before arriving with students to allow for effective preplanning. During the visit, pick up maps, schedules, and any other information that will help you plan the day effectively. (Note: If you cannot visit before the trip, much of this information may be accessible online.)
- Talk to your principal or school administrator about bus reservations and entry fees several months before the trip. Some locations may book up quite quickly.
- Send field trip notices home well in advance of the trip. Many districts have a standard field trip permission form—check with your principal.
- Call the destination to ask about the lunch break procedure (lunch storage, seating area, etc.).
- Arrange for chaperones and prepare them for whatever activity you have planned for the trip. A brief meeting a few days in advance will be helpful. Critical items to cover:
  - importance of staying with students at all times
  - any health considerations for individual students
  - details of the learning activities
  - emergency procedures and contact information
  - class rules, expectations, and consequences
- Decide on a gift shop policy and share with students' families before the trip. Keep in mind that some gift shops are not able to accommodate 20–30 customers at a time. Decide if the time spent in the gift shop will take away from other experiences.
- Provide students with visuals of the site you will be visiting, in addition to restroom, lunch, and rest information. This preparation will reduce anxiety and allow students to ease into the experience.
- Review behavior expectations. If you will be taking a tour, practice asking relevant questions and listening attentively. Bring objects into the classroom before the trip so younger students can practice touching "carefully." Discuss the level of talking that is appropriate for different destinations, as well as how to communicate effectively with adults.

During the trip . . .

- Provide each adult with needed first-aid supplies and contact information.
- Carry a cell phone.
- Bring along student emergency cards and/or contacts.
- Identify where students should go if they become separated from the group.

- Allow sufficient time for eating and bathroom breaks.
- For very young students, attach school information to their clothing but do not include students' names. This could create a danger of someone luring the child away by "knowing" his or her name.

After the trip . . .

- Before departing, do several head counts. Leaving a student behind is not something you want to experience!
- Clean up any trash related to your lunch break.
- Check for all personal belongings.
- Check with chaperones for any student issues you should be familiar with before arrival at the school.

PLANNING ON-SITE FIELD TRIP ACTIVITIES

The activities in this book are based on a new understanding of how we can best structure field trips to meet both content goals and affective goals. Affective goals are focused on emotional needs, such as supporting a love of science, reading, or art, or helping to develop a respect for the out-of-doors. You might find the approaches in this book are very different from your own field trip experiences. Just as our understanding of classroom instruction has grown over the decades, so has our understanding of informal learning. For example, many educators find activity sheets a helpful way to focus student attention. In fact, many of the activities in this book utilize simple, open-ended activity sheets. However, research indicates these activity sheets should be short and open-ended, and should encourage students to look at the object or exhibit itself, not at the label (Griffin & Symington, 1997; Kisiel, 2003). It is also necessary to provide students with the opportunity to review all activity sheets they will be using before they actually reach the field trip site. In addition, it is important to balance self-directed learning with basic structure. Too much structure can take away from enjoyment, but too little structure can endanger content goals (Stronck, 1983). Pace and Tesi (2004) studied adult memories of field trips and found that those who were actively engaged retained more information from their trip.

The activities in this book provide examples of how to balance these two approaches successfully. We all like to have some say in what we learn! Students are no different. Research has shown that when students are intrinsically motivated, or guided by their own desire to learn, we can see greater learning gains (Covington, 1998; Csikszentmihalyi & Hermanson, 1995). The activities in this book are designed to allow for student choice and help support the development of this intrinsic motivation. Last, the activities in this book will provide you with ideas to spark the creation of your own original activities for your next visit.

DESIGNING SUPPORTIVE CLASSROOM ACTIVITIES

Carefully planned previsit and postvisit classroom activities can significantly enhance the impact a field trip has on students. For supporting activities to be truly successful, they must incorporate the same level of thought and care as the field trip activity itself.

Previsit Activities

These activities should not only prepare students for the content they will encounter but also for the logistics of the excursion itself. Early museum research indicates that student learning can be jeopardized by an environment that is exceptionally strange or novel (Falk, Martin, & Balling, 1978). This effect is much like what we understand about Maslow's (1962) hierarchy of needs. Maslow explains that students cannot achieve higher-level content gains if they are concerned about their basic needs and safety. Prepare students for aspects of the trip that may be especially overwhelming or distracting by sharing slides, images from the Internet, or simple photographs taken on an earlier visit. This preparation can increase student focus on the subsequent trip without taking away the enjoyment and excitement of such a special experience.

Vignette: A Challenging Situation

"Okay everyone, let's gather together here and get ready to visit the sculpture garden," Ms. Jones directs her fourth graders. "Does everyone have their clipboard and writing and drawing tools?"

"Yes," they answer in chorus, straining to look past their teacher into the garden.

"Okay, let's go. Remember, once you are in the garden, select whichever sculpture you want to focus on. Begin with a journal free-write and then start a sketch of what you see."

The students push past Ms. Jones, eager to select a sculpture. A couple of students find one that catches their interest and immediately get to work, but the majority of the group stop dead in front of a replica of Michelangelo's "David." Half of the class is giggling nervously and pointing. The others are trying to appear uninterested but still jockey for position around the front of the statue. Ms. Jones tries to encourage students to begin their independent investigations but finds herself dealing with behavioral issues and inappropriate language instead. The carefully planned, self-directed exploration tumbles into chaos. Ms. Jones sighs and wonders what she could have done to ensure a more productive day.

Solution:

The presence of nudity in a gallery setting is to be expected. So is a varied set of responses from students, including giggling, pointing, and even anatomically based questions! One way Ms. Jones could have prepared for this "distraction" is to share images of some of the sculptures with the class prior to the visit, including the replica of "David." This would have provided a venue for some of the nervous giggling prior to the visit. In addition, it would have created a forum for discussion of nudity in works of art and her confidence that students can handle the nudity maturely, just like a real artist would. This most likely would not have eliminated all of the comments or glances, which are natural for young students, but would have reduced the novelty of the situation and assisted in getting students quickly back on track.

We know that students assimilate new information more easily if they have had prior exposure to the new content. While it is impossible to predict all content areas you and your students will encounter, preparing students with a general overview of the content highlighted by your field trip destination is key. Previsit activities will be most beneficial if they incorporate a sense of anticipation and preparation, as opposed to being designed as an exhaustive experience with the content. It is important to strive toward adequately preparing students while avoiding satiation or topic burnout.

LARGE GROUP CONSIDERATIONS

We all hope that on each field trip we will have enough chaperones to divide students into manageable groups of three to five. However, it is very common to end up a few chaperones short and with larger groups of students than originally planned for. The activities described in this book can be adjusted to be appropriate for large groups of students as well as smaller groups. One method is to take an activity originally written as an independent investigation and revise it to be a collaborative project instead. This will help large groups work together in a smaller space. Also, creating class leaders to help you supervise by simply counting students at regular intervals, or to serve as the communicator to indicate when the group is moving from one space to the next, can help with logistical control. Giving students specific activities to accomplish can be a big help with keeping them on task, even in a large, chaotic group. Adequate preplanning is going to significantly help you manage your large group and ensure a quality learning experience for your students.

POSTVISIT ACTIVITIES

Following up with students after a field trip is just as important as previsit preparation. Appropriate postvisit activities will help to reinforce content, address any misconceptions or confusion that may have arisen from the trip, and encourage students with additional opportunities for exploring topics of interest. Many of the activities in the book have postvisit activities presented as a second part to the on-site experience.

Postvisit activities need not be complex to be effective. The following is a list of quick and easy postvisit activities that fit any classroom curriculum.

- Bind any activity sheets that students have completed into a class book. Students can elect representatives to visit other classrooms and share their discoveries with younger students, or place the book in the school library.
- Ask students to draw a picture or write a story about something they experienced on the field trip.
- If the field trip is a yearly occurrence, have students write a letter to next years' students about what to expect on the trip.
- Place students in groups and have each group create an advertisement or brochure highlighting the most important aspects of the field trip destination.
- Support students in writing letters to the field trip site outlining the exhibitions or elements that were especially meaningful. Avoid general

thank-you notes that don't reinforce content. Ask students to focus on something specific from the exhibit.

- Lead a group discussion centered on students' questions related to the field trip, and design a strategy for answering each student's question through library research, contacting the field trip site, or consulting the Internet.

Whatever you choose, it is critical that the postvisit activity connect well with the on-site task students were responsible for completing. Closure is an important part of any lesson, including a field trip!

TAPPING INTO PREDESIGNED PROGRAMMING

This book is focused on activities for you to implement at a site with little or no programming already in place. However, many informal learning sites have a very rich offering of programming that can go a long way to creating a deeper learning experience for students. These might include guided tours, hands-on classes, bags or carts of touchable materials, and even the opportunity to venture behind the scenes and see researchers at work. Some of these are free, others are fee based. During preplanning, find out what programming the field trip site offers and check on any fees. Be sure to allow enough time to request reservations or secure necessary funding.

CONCLUSION

Planning a successful field trip is similar to planning a successful classroom activity. You'll need to be aware of your resources, your grade-level content standards, and your students' personal abilities and interests, just as with any other lesson plan. The main difference with an off-site field trip is that you will also need to learn how to best balance the novel with the familiar and the challenging with the comfortable, in order to create an experience that students will treasure for a lifetime. Creating relevant experiences for our students is a critical factor in creating quality learning opportunities. The following chapters will provide suggested activities that will help you meet this goal.

2

Active Investigators

Science Explorations

Current research, national standards documents, and even national tests indicate a need for authentic, inquiry-based experiences for elementary students. Tapping into resources outside the school environment, such as museums, zoos, and aquariums, is one way educators can make this happen even with limited resources in their own schools. In fact, many national science education organizations strongly support this connection as a way to strengthen science programs in the schools. These connections include drawing from resources such as field trips and structured outreach programs to professional development offerings and curricular materials (National Science Resources Center, National Academy of Sciences, & Smithsonian Institution, 1997; National Science Teachers Association, 1998).

PROVIDING INQUIRY-BASED EXPERIENCES: GOALS AND CHALLENGES

The National Science Education Standards show the impact an inquiry-based approach to science can have on students (National Research Council, 1996). Focusing on inquiry not only allows students to better understand the work of actual scientists, but helps them develop their critical thinking skills and problem-solving abilities. Inquiry is an active process by which students take the lead and move through scientific investigations based on their own questions and collection of their own data. The inquiry process includes

- making observations
- posing personally relevant questions

- examining existing information sources
- planning investigations
- gathering data using appropriate tools
- analyzing that data
- proposing explanations for student discoveries
- communicating the results of investigations

(National Research Council, 1996, p. 23)

Taking an inquiry-based approach in the classroom is a way to break down the work of actual scientists and bring it into the classroom. It allows for creativity, a quick change of direction, and even unexpected discoveries. Inquiry focuses on critical thinking and the process by which students come to conclusions. Not simply memorizing the right answer, inquiry focuses on skills that are directly in line with a successful career in the sciences. Figure 2.1 provides several publications that can be helpful in creating inquiry-focused experiences in your own classroom.

Any educator knows that creating a high-quality science experience in the classroom goes well beyond simply knowing what to do. It also requires access to appropriate resources. The research is clear that students need hands-on, constructivist-based science experiences (National Science Resources Center, National Academy of Sciences, & Smithsonian Institution, 1997) and most teachers are eager to provide these experiences. However, authentic tools, objects, specimens, and connections with natural phenomena can be in short supply in some districts and especially within our urban classrooms (Huinker, 1996). While many teachers have found a way to bring science alive in their classrooms by digging deep into their own pockets, writing grants, or learning how to tap into community resources, others still face limited resources, limited storage sites, outdated curriculum, and logistical issues of materials management in year-round schools and shared classroom space.

Thankfully, many of these challenges are not without possible solutions. Informal learning sites can be a source of helpful science materials based on the latest discoveries and may even provide objects on temporary loan, simplifying logistics of material storage and relieving cost considerations. Perhaps most important, though, these are places where teachers and students can visit and interact with scientific phenomena actively and in line with the work of true scientists.

MAKING CONNECTIONS: INFORMAL LEARNING SITES AND SCIENCE

Aquariums, Zoos, Animal Rehabilitation Centers

Though a visit to the local zoo or aquarium might be a common field trip, it is less common for students to take the opportunity for in-depth animal studies during this visit. The unique aspect of these sites is the presence of live animals, so it is important that students make these living, breathing, moving creatures the focus of their experience. These suggested activities present a chance for students to assume the role of wildlife biologists by identifying the animals they encounter and recording information in line with the work of scientists.

Figure 2.1   Additional Inquiry Resources

Learning and Assessing Science Process Skills

R. J. Rezba, C. S. Sprague, & R. L. Fiel
Kendall/Hunt Publishing (2003)
This publication provides guidance on structuring and assessing activities focused on skills associated with the inquiry process.

Inquiry-Based Learning Using Everyday Objects

A. E. Alvarado & P. R. Herr
Corwin Press (2003)
This publication offers pragmatic activities using easy-to-acquire objects with procedures well linked to best practices in inquiry-based investigations.

Inquiry Within: Implementing Inquiry-Based Science Standards in Grades 3–8, Second Edition

D. Llewellyn
Corwin Press (2007)
This publication provides detailed guidance on how to create inquiry-based experiences closely tied to national standards, together with theoretical support on the types of instructional techniques that can best support student inquiry.

Science for All Children

National Science Resources Center, National Academy of Science & Smithsonian Institution
National Academy Press (1997)
This publication provides both case studies of successful inquiry-based activities and practical guidance on transforming a science program at your school site.

K–2ND GRADE ACTIVITY: CHECK OUT THAT ANIMAL!

The first step for all scientists in conducting animal studies is the initial observation and identification of the animal they are studying. This activity provides students with the same opportunities.

Objectives

- Students will identify different animals using a developmentally appropriate field guide.
- Students will communicate discoveries orally.
- Students will communicate observations through written description.

National Science Education Standards (National Research Council, 1996)

- Standard A: Science as Inquiry
- Standard C: Life Science
- Standard G: Nature of Science

Procedures

1. Before the visit, provide students with examples of field guides that scientists or naturalists may use to help them identify different animals when they are out in

the field. Focus student attention on the format of the guide, specifically, that each entry has both a picture and key information about the animal.

2. In preparation for the visit, construct a "field guide" appropriate to students' developmental level and the animals they will encounter. There are many ways to structure your field guide.
   a. For first- and second-grade students, create paper journals with a different animal on each page. Provide a space for students to write a sentence or descriptive words for each animal they encounter.
   b. For kindergarten students, consider a "stick guide" (see Figure 2.2). The Stick Guide puts more emphasis on basic identification skills as well as oral communication with classmates. They take a bit more effort to make but are a huge hit with students! If you have enough adult help, you can have students dictate observations to be written directly on the sticks at the site. If not, these can be done back in the classroom.

3. During the visit, provide students with sufficient time to use their field guides both to identify the animals they encounter and to record their discoveries. It is best to wait until arrival at the site to pass out the field guides, to prevent a student from accidentally leaving his or her guide back in the classroom.

4. Back in the classroom after the visit, review with students which types of animals they encountered and any specific observations they made about the animal's appearance or behavior.

Figure 2.2   Creating a "Stick Guide"

- Locate black line masters of the different animals students will encounter. Make enough copies of each so there is one per student. There should be between five and ten different animal images depending on the length of your visit. Images should be about 3 square inches each.
- Roughly cut each image out. There is no need to follow lines. Rather, just cut the image into a more manageable size.
- Locate enough tongue depressors so there is one for each picture, or 5–10 for each student. Using a small-bore drill, drill a hole at the end of each.
- Using a hot glue gun, glue one picture on each tongue depressor at the end without the hole.
- Sort the different animals into piles so you have one pile for each student and each pile has one of each animal.
- Put the sticks in each pile on their own binder ring and tightly clasp the ring.

Evaluation Rubric

	No Credit	Credit
Field Guide Usage	There is no attempt to utilize field guides in conjunction with observations.	Student makes an attempt to identify animals using their field guide. This includes some writing within written guides (Grades 1–2) and manipulation of the stick guide (kindergarten).

Extension

Provide students with simple field guides focused on the bugs, birds, or plants within their own school yard and encourage them to conduct an investigation on their own during lunch, recess, or another designated outdoor time.

3RD–5TH GRADE ACTIVITY: HABITAT AND HOME

Many animal researchers spend a lot of time recording observations while in the field (the natural habitat of the animal) and away from a lab. During these observations, scientists will often note how the animal interacts with the habitat, such as where it finds food or seeks shelter. This activity allows students to make a similar analysis of animal habitat (see the vignette at the end of this chapter).

Objectives

- Students will identify the elements necessary for a healthy habitat.
- Students will analyze the habitat of an animal housed at the zoo, aquarium, or rehabilitation center.
- Students will make recommendations on how to improve the habitat.

National Science Education Standards
(National Research Council, 1996)

- Standard A: Science as Inquiry
- Standard C: Life Science

Procedures

1. Before the visit, discuss with students the critical elements of an animal's habitat that help it survive. At the minimum, these should include food, shelter, and water. However, students may brainstorm and identify a number of other elements they feel are critical. For example, behavioral enrichment, or mental stimulation for animals, is currently in the forefront of many zoo exhibit reforms. Once general elements of a healthy habitat are identified, students will be placed in groups and will select an animal for their study.

2. In preparation for the visit, it will be necessary to get a list of the animals that students will encounter during the trip. It is from this list that students will either select their study animal or have one assigned to them. Create for each student a research journal that provides space for students to take observational notes during the trip. There should be space for both making sketches and recording narrative notes.

3. During the visit, work with parent chaperones to help each group locate the exhibit space of their assigned animal. Working as a group, they will conduct an analysis of the habitat. Specifically, they will be trying to determine if the basic habitat needs as discussed in class are met within the exhibit space. They should record all elements of the group discussion. If possible, provide students with disposable cameras or select one person to take images of each habitat with a digital camera. These images can be used within students' final projects.

4. Back in the classroom, provide students with poster boards in order to create a final presentation. On the poster board, students will need to first identify the animal and provide sketches or photos of the habitat they observed. Next, they will need to provide an analysis of the habitat. Were basic needs met? Were enrichment needs met? If there were needs that were not met, students need to make suggestions for improving the space. These suggestions should be a combination of drawings and narrative description. These posters will be the piece that is formally assessed.

Evaluation Rubric

Final Project	1	2	3
Data Presentation	Information is presented inaccurately and/or limited information is presented.	Some information is presented accurately, but there is limited information and some errors.	Information is presented accurately and a rich amount of description is present.
Conclusions	Student's conclusions are not supported by the data.	Some of student's conclusions are supported by the data, others are not based on observations.	Student's conclusions are well rooted in observation data, with no unsupported conclusions.
Neatness/ Preparedness	Student's project shows little effort in the areas of neatness or advanced preparation.	Student's project demonstrates some advanced planning and effort in the area of neatness and presentation.	Student's final project is neat, well planned, and demonstrates a high degree of preparedness.

Extension

Students may decide to draft recommendations into a letter that can be shared with the zoo or wildlife park. This activity may be more effective with smaller institutions with intimate ties to the community. Work with students to draft a respectful letter, taking into account realities such as limited budgets. Perhaps even offer volunteer services where appropriate to make these suggestions easier to implement.

Helpful Web Sites

These Web sites provide the opportunity to "visit" a zoo or aquarium from the classroom, exploring exhibits and learning animal facts.

Birch Aquarium Online Activities
http://aquarium.ucsd.edu/Education/Learning_Resources

Monterey Bay Aquarium
http://www.mbayaq.org

San Diego Zoo
http://www.sandiegozoo.org

Smithsonian National Zoological Park
http://nationalzoo.si.edu

Outdoor Areas

You need not pay admission to have access to quality science experiences off campus. The local shoreline, a park, even a vacant lot can serve as settings for student-centered investigations. Conducting a biological census, or species count, of plants or animals is a great way for students to appreciate nature in their own community. The wealth of life even the most urban areas can support can be surprising. One way to ensure that these natural areas are preserved is by preparing students for positive interaction with their surroundings. Review rules about not harming plants or animals and for identifying what types of things are appropriate for "collecting" and which should simply be observed in their natural habitat.

K–2ND GRADE ACTIVITY: LOOK AT WHAT I FOUND!

Students love to collect things, from shells and rocks to sticks and seed pods. Scientists like to collect, too, but they are careful to collect lots of important information along with the natural item. This information helps them later when they are studying what they discovered. Encouraging students to record discovery data along with their find helps them take a first step in building a scientific collection in line with that of real researchers.

Objectives

- Students will collect five natural objects from a nearby outdoor area.
- Students will record where the object was found, the date, and the time.

National Science Education Standards
(National Research Council, 1996)

- Standard A: Science as Inquiry
- Standard B: Physical Science
- Standard C: Life Science
- Standard D: Earth and Space Science
- Standard E: Science and Technology
- Standard G: Nature of Science

Procedure

1. Before the activity, explain to students that it is important for scientists to be gentle with nature. Not all things they discover will be okay to take back to the classroom. Have them brainstorm which natural items are appropriate for "collecting" and which are not. Also, spend time deciphering between natural objects and manufactured items.

2. Also review the importance of recording information about where an object was found and when it was found. For example, a lion found in Africa is not that unusual. A lion found in Newark, New Jersey, is *very* unusual.

3. Take students on a walk through a natural area and ask them to point out what types of birds, bugs, and/or plants they find. Each student will have five paper bags to collect natural items such as feathers, rocks, and leaves.

a. For kindergarten students, have them dictate the location for each item (an adult can write this on the bag).

b. For first- and second-grade students, have them write the time and location on the bag themselves.

4. Back in the classroom, help create a center showcasing each student's discoveries with the accompanying data. Lead a discussion of how the information they have collected provides more insight than if they had just collected the object without taking notes. What conclusions can students draw based on the information that was collected?

Evaluation Rubric

	1	2	3
Data Collection	Student labels an object with collection data as developmentally appropriate.	Student labels 2–3 objects with collection data as developmentally appropriate.	Student labels 4–5 objects with collection data as developmentally appropriate.

Extension

If possible, provide students with disposable cameras for recording discoveries that cannot be brought back to the classroom, such as trees or birds.

3RD–5TH GRADE ACTIVITY: HOW MANY?

In order to better understand the entire ecology of a natural area, scientists will often conduct surveys, or counts of the different species that live within a natural area and the abundance of each of these plants or animals. Students should also describe the physical features of the study area. This activity will give students the opportunity to conduct their own habitat survey.

Objectives

- Students will measure a transect for data collection.
- Students will identify and count the species within a transect.
- Students will describe physical features of the environment.
- Students will compile their data into a final report.
- Students will share their discoveries with their classmates.

National Science Education Standards (National Research Council, 1996)

- Standard A: Science as Inquiry
- Standard C: Life Science
- Standard D: Earth and Space Science
- Standard G: Nature of Science

Procedures

1. Explain that when scientists study an area, they often cannot count every plant or animal that can be found over miles and miles. Instead, they take counts in a small section or transect and then make generalizations about numbers in the whole space based on this transect. Donald Silver's "One Small Square" book series is a child-friendly device for sharing the concept of transects.

2. Take students to a natural area and assign them transects, or sections within the space, for their investigation. One way to do this is to place students in a straight line. Have one student stop after taking three steps, another after taking six steps, another after taking nine steps, etc. Each stopping point will mark a student's transect.

3. Create a grid for investigation by stretching a coat hanger into a square shape. Students will record whatever they see in the square on a data sheet provided. Students do not need to know the names of each species they find; simple descriptions and sketches (i.e., black beetle, tiny green bug) will provide enough detail to teach the idea of biodiversity. A sample data sheet is provided at the end of the chapter (Data Sheet 1).

4. Back in the classroom, have students compare their data. Which area had the highest diversity (largest number of different plant/animal species)? Why do they think this is so?

5. Have students create a final project showcasing their discoveries. They can then arrange to share this project with students at another grade level. Projects can be a display board, a multimedia presentation, or a special pamphlet. This is the piece that will be formally evaluated.

Evaluation Rubric

Final Project	1	2	3
Data Presentation	Survey data are presented inaccurately; calculations contain errors.	Some survey data are presented accurately; there are some calculation errors.	Survey data are presented accurately; there are no calculation errors.
Conclusions	Student's conclusions are not supported by the data.	Some of student's conclusions are supported by the data, others are not based in observations.	Student's conclusions are well rooted in observational data; there are no unsupported conclusions.
Oral Presentation	Student is not prepared.	Student is somewhat prepared, but at times hesitates or requires assistance from peers or teacher.	Student is well prepared and does not need assistance.

Modification

Another transect option is to have students walk together in a straight line for a set distance. They should record everything they see within a foot of this line. This is a way to include larger things that would not fit into the coat hanger square as well as accommodate full-group instruction.

Helpful Web Sites

These sites provide opportunities for students to work with real data, as well as contribute to national research projects.

Cornell Lab of Ornithology
http://www.birds.cornell.edu

National Weather Service
http://www.weather.gov/om/reachout/kidspage.shtml

Web Weather for Kids
http://www.eo.ucar.edu/webweather

Natural History Museums

Natural history museums are known for their eclectic mix of nature and culture. Each museum will have elements and exhibits unique to its collections, the objects stored behind the scenes that researchers study and protect. Dioramas, taxidermied animals set in realistic environments, are one exhibit style common in a variety of different natural history museums. They can be found in the oldest of institutions, such as the Field Museum of Chicago, as well as the newest, such as the Draper Museum of Natural History in Cody, Wyoming.

K–2ND GRADE ACTIVITY: A PERFECT PICTURE

Words are not the only way that scientists communicate. Sometimes an illustration or a diagram is truly the best way to illustrate a scientific discovery or phenomenon. In creating scientific illustrations, the emphasis is on accuracy over aesthetics. Providing students with the opportunity to show what they know through illustrations is not only in line with the work of practicing scientists, but also allows for students who may struggle with literacy to use an alternative avenue to demonstrate their understanding of the content.

Objectives

- Students will observe preserved animals in a museum exhibit.
- Students will record observations through scientific illustration.
- Students will record habitat and environment through scientific illustration.
- Students will label scientific illustrations as developmentally appropriate.

National Science Education Standards
(National Research Council, 1996)

- Standard A: Science as Inquiry
- Standard C: Life Science
- Standard G: Nature of Science

Procedures

1. Before the visit, acquaint students with the process of scientific illustration. Many scientists include scientific illustrations in their research publications. Scientific illustrations are also used in textbooks, or to capture the beauty of something that must be left in the wild. Encourage students to look through books in the class library to identify examples of scientific illustration.

2. At the museum, provide each student with a clipboard, a small pouch of colored pencils and a regular pencil, and plenty of blank, white paper. Place students in small groups and have each group select an animal display they would like to focus on for their project. Remind students to focus on the animals themselves and not what they may know from books or movies.

3. Ask students to label their drawing in line with their language arts skills. Some students may benefit from a word bank and others may be able to label without assistance. Chaperones can also help students correctly label each illustration. Questions that may direct their labeling include the following:
   a. Can they identify the adults in the grouping?
   b. Can they identify the juveniles ("teenagers")?
   c. Can they tell the difference between the males and the females?
   d. What do they notice about the animals' habitat?

4. Back in the classroom, you can assemble all student illustrations into a class book that can be placed in the school library for other students to enjoy. Student illustrations will be the final assessment piece.

Evaluation Rubric

Illustration	1	2	3
Accuracy	Student's illustration is not based on the actual animal.	Student's illustration is partly accurate but also contains some inaccurate body parts, structures, or colors.	Student's illustration is an accurate representation of the animal.
Detail	Student's illustration is primarily an outline of shape and lacks any additional detail.	Student's illustration has some detail, but lacks many elements that are specific to the animal.	Student's illustration shows as much detail as possible; there are no obvious omissions.
Neatness	Student's illustration shows little care for neatness and is nearly illegible.	Student's illustration is fairly neat, though there are clear examples where student could have provided more effort.	Student's illustration is neatly presented, with no smudges, crossed-out items, or scribbles.

3RD–5TH GRADE ACTIVITY:
WHAT I KNOW … WHAT I THINK

Even if a scientist wanted to, it would be difficult to conduct observations every day, twenty-four hours a day. Everyone needs a chance to eat and sleep! Many times scientists might have to speculate as to what happened before they began their observation or what might happen after they are gone. Scientists do not want to make wild guesses with nothing to back them up. That is simply not science. Instead, they might make *inferences* or *predictions* that are logical guesses based on evidence they have observed or gathered from books and other data sources. This activity allows students to practice their inference and prediction skills.

Objectives

- Students will make observations of animal interaction.
- Students will infer what may have happened prior to their observation based on observable evidence.
- Students will predict what may happen next based on observable evidence.
- Students will compare/contrast inferences and predictions with their classmates.

National Science Education Standards
(National Research Council, 1996)

- Standard A: Science as Inquiry
- Standard C: Life Science
- Standard G: Nature of Science

Procedures

1. Students will take on the role of a field biologist and conduct "observations" of the animals within the dioramas. Before the visit, acquaint them with scientific research through online research journals or books focused on the work of science researchers.

2. At the museum, place students in groups based on the animal they want to use for the observation. While students will be encouraged to discuss the diorama with their group, they will complete the writing assignment on their own.

3. During the visit, explain that most dioramas are designed as a snapshot in time. It will be the students' job to explain, through inference and prediction, what is going on in the diorama, what happened just prior to this snapshot, and what they anticipate will happen next. Encourage students to use rich description and detail. A thoughtful entry might read like this:

   Before: *"The zebras were starving and were trying to eat all the grass they could. They took turns looking for danger. There are many predators in Africa."*

   Right Now: *"The male zebra stares at the approaching lion. The other zebras stay close. They know the lion is coming and try to protect themselves."*

   Future: *"The zebras were lucky. The male zebra kicked the lion and it went away. The other zebras could keep eating."*

4. Once back in the classroom, allow students to partner and compare their journal entries. During their discussion, have them focus on how they developed their inference of the past as well as their prediction for the future. Journals will then be collected by the teacher for evaluation.

Evaluation Rubric

Journals	1	2	3
Plausibility of Prediction(s)	Student predictions are not well supported.	Student predications are somewhat logical, not entirely based on observations.	Student predictions are logical and well connected to observations made at the site.
Plausibility of Inference(s)	Student inferences are not well supported.	Student inferences are somewhat logical, but not entirely based on observations.	Student inferences are logical and well connected to observations made at the site.
Participation in Group Discussion	Student did not actively discuss project with partner.	Student made some effort to discuss project with partner, but was at times off task or distracted.	Student was actively engaged in discussion with partner regarding the project.

Modification

If class contains a number of English learners or students who struggle with literacy, the assignment can be completed as a group rather than individually.

Helpful Web Sites

These well-known natural history museums provide a range of resources to learn more about natural history topics, collections, and exhibits.

American Museum of Natural History
http://www.amnh.org

California Academy of Sciences
http://www.calacademy.org/naturalhistory

The Field Museum
http://www.fieldmuseum.org

Natural History Museum of Los Angeles County
http://www.nhm.org

Botanical Gardens/Arboretums

Many students grow up without a backyard of their own or access to a local park. Before a trip to a botanical garden, their experience with plants may be limited to the dandelions growing between sidewalk cracks or the vegetables they eat for dinner. Students who do have access to natural areas, either on their own home property or in surrounding areas, might need some prompting to recognize the amazing biology and diversity of plants. The following activities build on the ideas within the section on Outdoor Areas but will add in some specific "plant watching" and geology skills.

K–2ND GRADE ACTIVITY: USING MORE THAN EYES

While a practicing scientist will rarely use a scavenger hunt to guide his or her research, a scientist will be careful to rely on a variety of senses, such as sight, smell, and touch, throughout the data collection process. This activity will help students learn to rely on senses other than sight to experience the world around them.

Objectives

- Students will use a variety of senses to collect information of the surrounding environment.
- Students will record the information they gather through words and pictures.

National Science Education Standards (National Research Council, 1996)

- Standard A: Science as Inquiry
- Standard B: Physical Science
- Standard C: Life Science
- Standard D: Earth and Space Science

Procedure

1. Before the visit, let students know that they will be using a scavenger hunt to help them explore the gardens they visit. Explain that with the scavenger hunt, there will be many possible correct answers and you hope they use the time to explore things that are interesting to them.

2. On the day of the visit, provide students with a clipboard, pencil, and a brief, open-ended scavenger hunt. The research presented in Chapter 1 reminds us that any activity sheet should be brief and allow for multiple correct answers focused on the object, rather than what might be written in a tiny label or text panel. For example:
   a. Find a yellow flower. Draw its picture here.
   b. Locate a water feature.
   c. Find moist, rich soil.
   d. Find something with a strong scent.
   e. Draw a plant that felt good to touch.
   f. Find a very shady spot. Draw a map to get there.

3. During the visit, provide scaffolding as necessary to support completion of the scavenger hunt.

4. Back in the classroom, compile scavenger hunt sheets into a class book that can serve as a reminder of the visit. Encourage students to look through the book and see the many different responses their classmates provided for the same questions.

Evaluation Rubric

	No Credit	Credit
Scavenger Hunt Activity Sheet	Minimal effort is demonstrated. Few items are identified. Minimal data are recorded.	Significant effort is demonstrated. Student has made an effort to identify the majority of items and record data.

Modification

For younger students or students who may struggle with language, you may want to use illustrations to guide the scavenger hunt rather than words.

3RD–5TH GRADE ACTIVITY: ALL ABOUT THE ENVIRONMENT

When researchers are working in the field, it is important for them to collect as much information as possible, including information that goes beyond the focus of the project. Scientists studying plants will need to record data about the surrounding soil, weather patterns, and animal life to get a complete picture of how the plants they are studying interact with a broader environment.

Objectives

- Students will identify a plant to be at the focus of their site analysis.
- Students will describe the surrounding geology of the area.
- Students will record seasonal and weather information.
- Students will create a scientific illustration of their selected plant.
- Students will explain how the plant is well suited for its environment.

National Science Education Standards
(National Research Council, 1996)

- Standard A: Science as Inquiry
- Standard B: Physical Science
- Standard C: Life Science
- Standard D: Earth and Space Science
- Standard E: Science and Technology
- Standard G: Nature of Science

Procedures

1. Before the visit, provide each student with a science journal. The science journal can be any format as long as there are lined pages for writing as well as blank pages for drawing. Within the front cover of the journal, attach a checklist for the information you expect each student to record during their visit. This will help students to collect all the required information for the project. For example:
   a. What is the weather today?
   b. Is the area sunny, shady, or both?

  c. Describe the soil.
  d. Is there water nearby?
  e. What plants surround your target plant?
  f. Are there animals nearby?
  g. Create a scientific illustration of the target plant.

2. At the site, allow students to spread out (consistent with supervision needs) and select a work area for their data collection. Provide students with plenty of time to record all needed information in their journals. It may be helpful to provide a few colored pencils to assist with the scientific illustration and a clipboard to make writing without a desk easier.

3. Back in the classroom, meet briefly with small groups of students to discuss their data. Guide them in determining how the surrounding environment contributes to the plants' survival—from soil to the amount of sun. Encourage them to learn from each other and compare their data with classmates. Practicing scientists also work together and learn from each other's data.

4. Last, provide students with the opportunity to create an individual final project outlining the data they collected and their conclusions as to how the environment and their plant species were a perfect match. The final project might be a poster, oral presentation, multimedia project, or a written report. This project will be the final assessment piece.

Evaluation Rubric

Final Project	1	2	3
Accuracy	Student's project is not based in information from the field trip.	Student's project is partly accurate but also contains some inaccurate information.	Student's project accurately summarizes key information about the target plant and surrounding environment.
Neatness	Student's project shows little care for neatness.	Student's project is fairly well presented, though there are clear examples where student could have provided more effort.	Student's project is neatly presented, with attention to detail.

Helpful Web Sites

These sites, linked to botanical gardens and arboretums, provide general botanical information, teaching resources, as well as general exhibit information.

Cleveland Botanical Garden
http://www.cbgarden.org

The Huntington Library, Art Collections, and Botanical Gardens
http://www.huntington.org

The National Garden
http://nationalgarden.org/national_garden.html

The United States National Arboretum
http://www.usna.usda.gov/SiteMap_USNA.html

ALSO CONSIDER . . .

Other field trip options to support science learning include

Science Centers: These institutions are usually dedicated to providing hands-on, student-centered exhibits and displays. The types of exhibitions can vary widely from one science center to another. Some science centers have exhibitions that feature live animals or taxidermy displays, so some of the activities described above will be appropriate. Science centers also often focus considerably on physical sciences and may provide a number of experiences where students initiate scientific phenomena by pressing a button or pulling a lever. A great way to structure student experiences in this space is to ask students to make predictions prior to engaging with an exhibition and record in a science journal both the predictions and what occurred.

Nature or Visitor Centers: These locations are often staffed by eager and helpful interpreters who will be instrumental in supporting your visit. Plan on information focused specifically on the local area presented on a medium to small scale. These locations often have a number of opportunities to handle and interact with actual objects and specimens.

Science Professionals: From visits to local doctors or dentists to a behind-the-scenes tour at a local university, going directly to the source of active science is an excellent way for students to gain insight into the large variety of people who use science in their everyday work.

Planetariums: Visits to these institutions usually involve a set program of viewing the night sky and often additional programming led by staff or volunteers. While a planetarium visit may not require the design of specific on-site activities, preparation and follow-up will still be critical to creating a successful experience.

Bakeries/Restaurants: Anyone who can cook knows that creating an excellent dish is an exercise in science. From the chemical reactions of mixed ingredients to issues in nutrition and health, visits to eateries can demonstrate to students the presence of science in their everyday lives.

Law Enforcement Agencies: Television has made the science of crime investigation and forensics everyday conversation. Check with your local law enforcement agency to see if a crime lab visit, or perhaps a visit from a forensic scientist, is possible.

Vignette: Investigation at the Zoo

"Ooooo... that tiger is WHITE and BLACK!"

"But the rest are orange and black... they look the same," Julie corrected her classmate.

"Take a closer look, Julie—do their stripes all look alike?" the teacher redirected.

Rosa piped in, "No! That one has thicker stripes. It's a yuckier orange than the other ones, too."

"Yuckier?" the teacher attempts to clarify.

"Well ... it's not that pretty orange, it's, ummmm ..."

"It's more dull!" shouts Carly, attempting to help Rosa in her vocabulary search.

"What do you think, Tyrone?" asked the teacher.

"I'm not looking at the stripes," he answered. "I'm looking for its food source."

"Excellent—you remember we discussed that as a critical habitat need."

"I don't think it has any food!" screams Tara.

"Okay, we might not see any right now, but is there evidence that there was food here earlier?" the teacher tries to clarify.

"There's an empty bowl there! They must have already eaten their breakfast," Tyrone offers.

"That's an excellent observation, Tyrone. Okay class, let's all focus our attention on the tiger's habitat. Do you feel its basic needs are being met? I'll keep an eye on our class thermometer while you are working."

The students try to get comfortable for the next stage of the activity and prepare to take notes in their science journals.

Data Sheet 1 Species Survey

What I Discovered!

Investigator:_____   Date:_____

Location:_____   Weather:_____

Animal Species (Name or Description):   Sketch:

_____

_____

_____

_____

_____

Plant Species (Name or Description):   Sketch:

_____

_____

_____

_____

Additional Observations:

_____

_____

_____

3

Language Alive

Language Arts Explorations

Language arts is an academic area that pervades every aspect of the school curriculum as well as everyday experiences. Current reform efforts emphasize the importance of building student skills in the area of literacy to support later success in life (U.S. Department of Education, 2004). Always considered a key component of the classroom curriculum, success in the area of language arts has now become a critical classroom priority. Supporting student success in the language arts requires providing opportunities for students to employ language arts skills within authentic settings. With the realization of the importance of context to building language skills (National Research Council, 1999), learning to connect field trip destinations to literacy building is a logical step.

LANGUAGE ARTS ALL AROUND

A quality language arts curriculum is one that provides students with real-world opportunities to employ reading, writing, and oral language skills. Language arts activities placed within a personally relevant and authentic context are critical to developing literacy skills in a diverse student body. A balanced literacy program involves more than classroom resources; it also connects to the home and the community (Frey, Lee, Tollefson, Pass, & Massengill, 2005).

Reading itself is a process students may do for enjoyment, as part of an assignment, or to gather critical information. Tapping into field trip opportunities provides a wealth of reading in line with real-world applications, a significant element of successful reading instruction (Guthrie, Wigfield, & Vonsecker, 2000).

Providing literacy-rich environments for young children and connecting language arts to everyday situations (Novick, 2000) is a need that field trip experiences can fill. In addition, a field trip experience provides opportunities to read nonfiction as well as short text, important to the development of overall student literacy (Harvey, 2002).

Making writing activities the focus of a field trip not only provides experience in line with professional application (Reed, 1996) but also gives students the opportunity to insert their own voice and experience, sharing information that they find personally relevant (MacCleod, 2004). Again, even short text, as a student might complete during a busy field trip, plays an important role in language arts development.

From reading labels to oral discussion with peers, there is a wealth of opportunities on a field trip for students to fine-tune their language arts skills. Perhaps the most important aspect of language arts experiences within a field trip environment is the real-world connection and linkages to professional practice that demonstrate to students just how deeply literacy pervades each aspect of our lives.

MAKING CONNECTIONS: INFORMAL LEARNING SITES AND LANGUAGE ARTS

Libraries and Bookstores

Building a familiarity with literature is one component of quality language arts instruction. A local library or bookstore will provide a wealth of authors, titles, and genres to stimulate student curiosity and highlight the range of literature available to them.

For both destinations, special planning will be necessary. Visiting the space in advance will be critical in determining if there is room for a full class to visit and not interfere with customers. Some bookstores are large enough to accommodate several classes. Others will simply not be of an appropriate size. It will be important to call ahead or have a discussion with the manager to ensure the visit will be a welcome one. Explaining the tasks students will be doing can be helpful in assuring employees that the visit will be structured and organized. Reviewing appropriate handling and treatment of books within public spaces will also be necessary.

K–2ND GRADE ACTIVITY: FACT OR FICTION?

A large selection of books provides students with an engaging opportunity to compare and contrast works of fiction and nonfiction. This activity encourages students to compare and contrast two works of different genres.

Objectives

- Students will select a work of fiction and a work of nonfiction around a central theme.
- Students will compare and contrast a work of fiction and nonfiction with similar subject matter.

Standards for the English Language Arts* (National Council of Teachers of English & International Reading Association, 1996)

- Standard 1: Students read a wide range of print and nonprint texts.
- Standard 3: Students apply a wide range of strategies to comprehend, interpret, evaluate, and appreciate texts.

- Standard 4: Students adjust their use of spoken, written, and visual language to communicate effectively.

Procedures

1. Before the visit, review with students the difference between fiction and nonfiction or informational text. Provide examples from the classroom library to reinforce the discussion.

2. In preparation for the visit, place students in groups of four and provide each group with an open-ended activity sheet to help guide data collection. This sheet can take many formats, from a traditional Venn diagram structure of two intersecting circles, to a list of several tasks, such as, "Describe how the two books are similar."

3. During the visit, ask each group first to select a picture book as their fictional selection. Have them discuss as a group what they feel the central theme of the story is. Is it a story about a donkey? An imaginary trip to the moon? Nightmares? Once they have agreed upon several key themes of the book, they will need to search out a nonfictional counterpart for their investigation. This counterpart should have a similar theme but be based in factual information. Parent chaperones, librarians, or bookstore clerks may need to assist younger students in locating books within the stacks.

4. Once both books have been selected, ask students to select a quiet space to work and complete their activity sheets. They will need to flip through the texts, evaluate the images, and read key excerpts in order to identify differences and similarities. Provide adult scaffolding as appropriate for students' ability levels. If possible, check out the different books that were at the focus of the study to support later discussion in the classroom.

5. Back in the classroom, arrange for students to communicate the results of their exploration. For younger children, this might be best arranged as a whole-class experience, with each group taking a chance to present. For older students, pairing up different groups and asking them to share their results with each other in a cooperative group format is an option.

6. At the end of the project, the activity sheets will be collected and scored as an assessment piece.

Evaluation Rubric

	1	2	3
Comparison Activity Sheet	Little is completed, and/or little effort is shown.	There is some information comparing and/or contrasting the two publications.	The two publications are compared and contrasted in detail.

Modification

Parent chaperones or even older students can support younger students in the use of technology to gather author information as well as assist with locating publications in the shelves. Students whose writing skills are still developing may want to use a combination of sketches and words to complete the activity sheet.

Source: Standards for the English Language Arts, by the International Reading Association and the National Council of Teachers of English, Copyright 1996 by the International Reading Association and the National Council of Teachers of English. Reprinted with permission. http://www.ncte.org/about/over/standards/110846.htm

3RD–5TH GRADE ACTIVITY: ALL ABOUT AUTHORS!

Bookstores and libraries provide students with access to multiple works by a single author. This provides the opportunity to understand the style of a single author as well as how their work has changed, or not changed, over time (see the vignette at the end of this chapter).

Objectives

- Students will review multiple fiction works from one author, looking for common themes, writing style, or characters.
- Students will complete an activity sheet highlighting their favorite work and why it is their favorite.

Standards for the English Language Arts (National Council of Teachers of English & International Reading Association, 1996)

- Standard 1: Students read a wide range of print and nonprint texts.
- Standard 3: Students apply a wide range of strategies to comprehend, interpret, evaluate, and appreciate texts.
- Standard 4: Students adjust their use of spoken, written, and visual language to communicate effectively.
- Standard 7: Students conduct research on issues and interests by generating ideas and questions.

Procedures

1. Before the visit, review with students the concept that many children's authors have published more than one book. Share a familiar book with students and provide examples of several other books by the same author.

2. Lead a discussion of the common themes that can be found in many of the books, as well as how the author's style or subject matter may have changed over time. Arranging the books by publication year will facilitate student comparison of earlier works with later works.

    In preparation for the visit, place students in groups of four. Select a number of children's authors who have a large volume of published works. A school librarian or district literacy coach can be helpful with this step. Create an open-ended activity sheet that asks a few, specific questions about the author's body of work (see Data Sheet 2 at the end of the chapter for an example). Questions should be tailored to classroom curriculum, but examples include the following:
    a. How are the books similar?
    b. What are some differences you notice between several of the books?
    c. How is the earliest book different from the others?
    d. Are all the books published through the same publishing house?
    e. What is the timeframe for this author to publish a new book? One a year? Two a year?

3. When you arrive at the field trip location, have one person from each group blindly select a name by drawing a slip of paper from a hat or bowl. This will be their assigned author. Next, support students in locating the appropriate area in the stacks for them to begin their search. This is also an excellent opportunity to support students in using on-line card catalogs.

4. The second portion of the activity will be for students to select their favorite work by the author. This portion will be done independently, though several children may be working with the same book. Once students have made a selection, they are going to practice recording critical data mixed with personal opinion in order to communicate with their peers. On a separate data sheet, they should record the following information:
   a. Title
   b. Author
   c. Publisher and date
   d. ISBN number
   e. Three reasons why they recommend this book to other students

5. Back in the classroom, provide the opportunity for students to orally present their preference with other students. Then collect students' individual preference activity sheets for later assessment. These activity sheets can later be assembled into a class book to support future literature selections.

Evaluation Rubric

	1	2	3
Oral Discussion	Student does not participate in on-site discussion and exploration.	Student participates at times in on-site discussion and exploration, but at other times is off task.	Student actively participates in all aspects of the on-site exploration and discussion.
Personal Favorite Activity Sheet	Student demonstrates 1 of 3 criteria: • identifies focus author and relevant publication information; • identifies favorite work; • explains personal choice.	Student demonstrates 2 of the 3 criteria.	Student demonstrates all 3 criteria.

Extension

For a book report assignment, students can select several works from one author and focus their report on how the author's style has changed over time or has remained consistent.

Helpful Web Sites

These sites provide information on quality literature selections, using children's books within the curriculum and information on different authors.

Children's Book Council
http://www.cbcbooks.org

International Reading Association: Children's Literature and Reading Special Interest Group
http://www.csulb.edu/org/childrens-lit

The New York Public Library
http://kids.nypl.org/reading/recommended2.cfm?ListID=60

Museums

For these activities, the term *museum* applies to any genre of museum that contains exhibits, artifacts, or interactive experiences for the public to enjoy. From children's museums to museums of contemporary art, language is a critical component to supporting the visitor experience. This includes carefully written label copy, listening experiences, or oral discussion with employees or volunteers.

K–2ND GRADE ACTIVITY: I'M THE TEACHER

Many children love the opportunity to share a museum experience with a family member or friend. The chance to reteach provides reinforcement of content, aids in the learning process, and builds oral fluency. This activity allows students to share new information with their peers.

Objectives

- With the help of an adult chaperone, students will become experts about a specific object or exhibition.
- Students will use effective oral communication to "teach" a peer this new knowledge.

Standards for the English Language Arts (National Council of Teachers of English & International Reading Association, 1996)

- Standard 4: Students adjust their use of spoken, written, and visual language to communicate effectively.
- Standard 10: Students whose first language is not English make use of their first language to develop competency in the English language arts and to develop understanding of content across the curriculum.
- Standard 11: Students participate as knowledgeable, reflective, creative, and critical members of a variety of literacy communities.

Procedures

1. Before the visit, review the types of exhibitions students will encounter during the field trip. Select six exhibits that students would like to focus on for their peer-teaching activity. These six exhibit names should be written on slips of paper for later group selection.

2. In preparation for the visit, lead a class discussion of effective teaching techniques. How do they like to learn? How should important information be shared? Place students into six groups before the field trip.

3. At the site, ask a representative from each group to select an exhibition for the discussion. With the assistance of an adult chaperone or older student volunteer,

have students spend time studying the exhibit and becoming an expert in what the exhibit is teaching. Provide the means to take photos of the exhibit with a digital or disposable camera.

4. After sufficient time has been provided to learn about the exhibit, the class will reconvene. Each student group will then be paired with an additional group. The two groups will together visit both exhibitions, providing the opportunity for peer teaching.

5. One method of structuring this peer teaching is to pair each student from within one group with a partner from the other group. Though the two groups will move together through the exhibit space, the peer teaching will largely be on a one-to-one basis.

6. Back in the classroom, students will take turns sharing what they learned from their peer teacher as well as the techniques their peer teacher used that were particularly helpful. A sample answer might be the following:

> *"At the children's museum, I learned that it takes more than one firefighter to drive the fire truck. I like that Ramon spoke clearly and didn't mind answering my questions."*

Evaluation Rubric

	No Credit	Credit
Peer Teaching	Student does not participate or participates with a negative attitude.	Student participates in peer-teaching aspect of the lesson with enthusiasm.

Modification

For English learners, allow both the information gathering phase and the peer-teaching phase to incorporate a child's first language. This will assist in the most information being transferred from one student to another and support development of English fluency.

3RD–5TH GRADE ACTIVITY: THE PERFECT LABEL

Writing labels is not an easy task. Exhibit labels must be concise, grammatically correct, engaging, and relevant to a diverse audience. This activity allows students to practice writing skills as they consider all of these factors.

Objectives

- Students will select an exhibit for which they would like to create a new label.
- Students will gather information during the visit regarding the exhibit or object.
- Back in the classroom, students will work in pairs to draft a new label.

Standards for the English Language Arts (National Council of Teachers of English & International Reading Association, 1996)

- Standard 4: Students adjust their use of spoken, written, and visual language to communicate effectively.
- Standard 5: Students employ a wide range of strategies as they write and use different writing process elements appropriately.
- Standard 8: Students use a variety of technological and informational resources to gather and synthesize information and to create and communicate knowledge.
- Standard 12: Students use spoken, written, and visual language to accomplish their own purposes.

Procedures

1. Before the field trip, lead a discussion of how museums put a great deal of work into labels so they are interesting and readable to a diverse audience. Review how proper sentence structure, grammar, and clear writing are critical components of a well-written label.

2. In preparation for the visit, bring in some objects for sample label writing. As a class, construct a paragraph that would be an appropriate label for a museum setting. Inform students that during the field trip they will be collecting information about an object or an exhibit of their choice in order to create an original label back in the classroom.

3. During the visit, place students in pairs and provide each pair with a clipboard and lined paper for note taking. As students explore the museum, they will be selecting one exhibit or object they would like to use as the focus of their project. Then students will take notes about the object or exhibit, collecting enough data to create a label of their own. Labels may include information taken from existing labels as well as simple description based on students' own perceptions of the physical exhibit.

4. While students are working, either the teacher or a parent chaperone can circulate, taking photos of the selected exhibits with a disposable or digital camera. These images will accompany the finished label that students turn in for final assessment.

5. Back in the classroom, provide additional instruction on how to construct a clear, concise paragraph. Though there is much debate on the proper length of a museum label, a word count of fifty is a good target (Serrell, 1996). Students may need to see a visual sample to better visualize a length of fifty words.

6. Students should work in their pairs to create a rough draft of their label, using their notes as well as images of the exhibit to support their efforts. Once they are done with their rough drafts, they should partner with another pair of students. While working in this group of four, students can provide feedback to assist in the creation of a label that is clear, easy to read, and engaging.

7. When students are pleased with their final product, provide them with access to a classroom computer and word-processing program in order to create a finished product. Final labels can be displayed on a bulletin board alongside an image of the target exhibition. This final label will serve as the assessment piece.

Evaluation Rubric

	1	2	3
On-Site Participation	Student is off task.	At times, student actively participates in cooperative groups; at other times is off task and not working with the group.	Student is actively engaged in cooperative group work and note taking during the field trip.
Final Label	Student does not create a label or label does not address field trip content.	Final label shows effort, but has errors in writing and/or is not well connected to the focus exhibit or object.	Label is well written and well connected to the focus exhibit or object.

Modification

For students that struggle with literacy, the short length of the label will assist in making the task less daunting. However, these students may additionally benefit from a word bank and a partner to work with.

Helpful Web Site

This site provides helpful information on both understanding and creating museum labels.

Alaska State Museum: Label Writing Tips
http://www.museums.state.ak.us/Bulletin/labels1.html

Oral Presentations

Most communities are rich in opportunities to hear the spoken word. From a town council meeting to book reading at a local library, the opportunity to hear a carefully prepared speech is excellent for students still learning about oral communication skills. The most important step will be to identify a speaking engagement well matched to students' developmental level as well as the classroom curriculum. For example, the portion of a city hall meeting focused on building a new playground will be more engaging for second graders than a detailed discussion of accounting issues.

K–2ND GRADE ACTIVITY: LEARNING TO LISTEN

Oral presentations are a wonderful opportunity for younger students to practice listening skills. This activity also asks students to take part in a discussion back in the classroom to analyze how well the presentation matched the needs of the audience.

Objectives

- Students will practice listening skills during a formal presentation.
- In class discussion, students will critique the ability of the speaker to meet the needs of his or her audience.

Standards for the English Language Arts (National Council of Teachers of English & International Reading Association, 1996)

- Standard 4: Students adjust their use of spoken, written, and visual language to communicate effectively.
- Standard 5: Students employ a wide range of strategies as they write and use different writing process elements appropriately.
- Standard 9: Students develop an understanding of and respect for diversity in language use, patterns, and dialects across cultures, ethnic groups, geographic regions, and social roles.
- Standard 11: Students participate as knowledgeable, reflective, creative, and critical members of a variety of literacy communities.

Procedures

1. Before the visit, provide students with exposure to a formal presentation. This might be a video clip, an audio clip, or images from the Internet. After sharing, discuss with students the different aspects of the presentation that made it successful. Did the speaker have a strong voice? Did he or she share information that was interesting and engaging?

2. In preparation for the visit, lead a discussion of proper listening etiquette. How can students show a speaker they are interested? When is the right time to raise hands and ask questions? What should they do with their bodies while they are listening?

3. Let students know that they will be attending a special presentation. They will need to demonstrate good listening skills during the presentation, both to display good manners and to be able to participate in a later classroom activity. During the presentation, they should consider what the presenter does especially well. Specifically, is the presentation well matched to the audience? They will be asked to share these opinions during a follow-up classroom discussion.

4. During the visit, monitor students to ensure they are displaying appropriate audience behavior. A visual signal can be agreed upon ahead of time to serve as a noninvasive reminder to students who are off task to behave appropriately. Supportive smiles will prompt on-task students to keep up the good work.

5. Back in the classroom, compliment students on being attentive and polite. Begin a discussion on the different aspects of the presentation that students thought were especially successful. In particular, discuss with students how effective they felt the speaker was in meeting the needs of the audience. Was the presentation well constructed for the attendees? Did the speaker seem to have a good connection with the audience?

6. In addition to discussing successful aspects of the presentation, lead a discussion of anything that could have improved the presentation. This is a good opportunity to reinforce for students what constructive criticism is, and the importance of identifying the many things someone does well in addition to highlighting areas for improvement. To conclude the discussion, take a class poll on how well students felt the presenter met the needs of the audience.

Evaluation Rubric

	1	2	3
Oral Presentation Response	Student is off task for both phases of the activity.	Student successfully participates in either the listening activity or the discussion. -OR- Student participates in both, but at a less than attentive level.	Student listens attentively during presentation and participates actively in follow-up discussion.

Extension

After students discuss how to create a presentation that is well matched to the listening audience, they can be assigned an age-appropriate oral presentation assignment to demonstrate this new understanding. Younger children may focus on simply sharing a special object or toy. Older students may be asked to do presentations based on content in the other academic areas.

3RD–5TH GRADE ACTIVITY: BEGINNING, MIDDLE, AND END

Older students are beginning to prepare longer, more detailed oral presentations of their own. This activity asks them to explore different portions of a formal presentation to determine criteria for a successful speech from beginning to end.

Objectives

- Students will analyze an oral presentation by critiquing at several key points during the speech.
- During class discussion, students will provide advice on how the presentation could have been more effective and write this advice in letter form.

Standards for the English Language Arts (National Council of Teachers of English & International Reading Association, 1996)

- Standard 4: Students adjust their use of spoken, written, and visual language to communicate effectively.
- Standard 9: Students develop an understanding of and respect for diversity in language use, patterns, and dialects across cultures, ethnic groups, geographic regions, and social roles.
- Standard 11: Students participate as knowledgeable, reflective, creative, and critical members of a variety of literacy communities.

Procedures

1. Before attending the presentation, review with students the three critical components of a successful presentation: an engaging beginning; a thoughtful, well-organized middle; and a conclusion with impact. Discuss the particular type of presentation students will be attending and lead a discussion of what they would expect from each section of the presentation.

2. In preparation for attending the presentation, remind students about appropriate listening etiquette. Also explain that they will need to pay close attention to the different portions of the presentation for later classroom discussion and an associated writing assignment. Address the fact that sometimes taking notes during a presentation is not appropriate, so they will want to use their best listening skills in order to retain critical information.

3. Circulate among students during the presentation, ensuring that they are displaying proper listening skills and polite engagement. It might help to take some notes on behalf of students to facilitate later discussion.

4. Back in the classroom, lead a class discussion of the presentation. The discussion should focus on how well the speaker performed at three key points within the speech: beginning, middle, and end. Students should share specifically what engaged them at the start. What was said that made them eager to hear the rest of the speech? In addition, they should discuss how well the speaker held their attention during the middle of the presentation. Did they find their attention wandering or were they actively engaged at each point? How did the ending of the presentation affect them? Did they find themselves leaving inspired or wanting to seek out similar experiences? As students share, comments can be written on the chalkboard or on poster paper to support students with creating their letters.

5. As a second follow-up activity, students will be asked to draft their thoughts into a letter. Though this letter will not actually be sent to the speaker, it should summarize what parts of the presentation were especially effective as well as any suggestions for improvement. Students should address the three parts of the presentation: beginning, middle, and end. They should ensure their letters provide a balance between compliments and constructive criticism. In addition, ask students to provide very specific information to support their position, rather than general statements such as, "It was good." These letters will serve as the final assessment piece of the activity.

Evaluation Rubric

	1	2	3
Student Letter	Student letter addresses only 1 of the 3 sections of the speech and/or does not address the needed criteria.	Student letter addresses only 2 of the 3 sections of the speech. -OR- Student letter addresses only positive or constructive elements for all 3 sections.	Student letter provides positive feedback as well as constructive suggestions as needed regarding the 3 focus sections of the speech.

Modification

   English learners may find that it is difficult to follow the nuances of a presentation due to new vocabulary or rapid speech. To support English learners, provide time to discuss the presentation with a peer before being asked to share their perceptions with the class. This preparation will also assist with the letter writing activity.

Helpful Web site

Toastmasters
   This organization's Web site provides tips for public speaking.
http://www.toastmasters.org/tips.asp

Outdoor Spaces

   Literacy development includes a focus on an ever-increasing interest in reading and writing for enjoyment and personal expression. Journals and diaries are an excellent way for students to develop literacy skills. Many educators already provide opportunities for personal journaling. Creating nature or environmental journals is an excellent way to integrate language arts across the curriculum authentically, as well as help students build new vocabulary.

K–2ND GRADE ACTIVITY: PLANT JOURNAL

Nature journals support the introduction of new vocabulary as well as support authentic integrations across the curriculum. In this activity, students make focused observations of a plant of their choice, either as a one-time investigation or recording changes over time.

Objectives

- Using a word bank with relevant terms, students will record observations about a single plant of their choice.
- Students will select an entry and read it aloud to their peers, explaining why the chosen entry is their favorite.

Standards for the English Language Arts (National Council of Teachers of English & International Reading Association, 1996)

- Standard 4: Students adjust their use of spoken, written, and visual language to communicate effectively.
- Standard 5: Students employ a wide range of strategies as they write and use different writing process elements.
- Standard 12: Students use spoken, written, and visual language to accomplish their own purposes.

Procedures

1. Before the visit, determine how many field trips to the particular location are reasonable. For example, if the field trip requires a bus, one visit may be all that is possible. If the focus is on a park within walking distance, several repeat visits can be made. Using these parameters as guides, determine ahead of time if you will expect a single, lengthy journal entry on a target plant or several short entries over a significant period of time.

2. In preparation for the visit, share published or Internet-based journal entries with students (see the Helpful Web Sites section for examples). Discuss the amount of detail and rich description within the different entries. Explain that journals are a place for factual information as well as thoughts and feelings about the field trip experience.

3. Provide students with composition books to serve as their journals. To facilitate the writing process, attach a word bank to the front cover of the journal. This word bank should include vocabulary appropriate for the field trip destination. *Dandelion* and *palm tree* might be important vocabulary for a school located in Florida. *Oak tree* and *maple tree* are critical vocabulary for a Vermont school. The focus during the visit will be to select a single plant for their observations.

4. During the visit, provide students with time to explore the space physically before sitting down to write. Younger students will need time to understand the environment before they capture it in written form. Once students have found a quiet place to sit and record their thoughts, it will be important to circulate and provide encouragement as necessary. Students who finish more quickly than their peers can take the opportunity to practice reading their entries aloud to another classmate who has finished. Or they might decide to create an additional entry on another plant.

5. After all journal entries have been completed—whether the assignment is a single entry or multiple entries over time—students will be asked to reflect on their work and share orally with their peers. After each student shares, provide the opportunity for peers to reflect on how this entry is similar to or different from their own. Did students notice different aspects of the same type of plant? Were there certain vocabulary words from the word bank that students used more frequently than others?

6. To complete the activity, lead a classroom discussion of how journaling is an important part of everyday life. What are some things students may want to write about? Collect the field trip journals as a final assessment piece. If possible, provide students with an additional composition book that can serve as a journal at home.

Evaluation Rubric

	1	2	3
Journal Entries	Student entries show little effort, with a minimal amount written.	Student entries show effort, but some lack necessary length and detail and/or show limited use of key vocabulary.	Student entries are detailed and rich, are of significant length, and utilize words within the word bank as appropriate.
Entry Reading	Student either does not read a journal entry or does so with limited effort.	Student reads a journal entry with some feeling, but is at times disengaged.	Student reads a journal entry in a strong voice and with excitement about the topic.

Modification

Depending on school policy, you may provide English learners with the opportunity to use a mixture of English and their native language during the journaling process. This will ensure students' thoughts are captured accurately, and thoughts can be translated at a later date. Students struggling with literacy may find that sketches and pictures can be used in addition to simple sentences.

3RD–5TH GRADE ACTIVITY: WHAT'S GOING ON TODAY?

Journals are an excellent opportunity for recording information over a period of time and then reflecting on how things may have changed. In this activity, students reflect on their journaling and create a final entry summarizing all of the data that have been recorded.

Objectives

- Students will record repeated observations of neighborhood spaces in a journal.
- Students will create a final entry summarizing the changes they have recorded over time.

Standards for the English Language Arts (National Council of Teachers of English & International Reading Association, 1996)

- Standard 4: Students adjust their use of spoken, written, and visual language to communicate effectively.
- Standard 5: Students employ a wide range of strategies as they write and use different writing process elements.
- Standard 12: Students use spoken, written, and visual language to accomplish their own purposes.

Procedures

1. Before the field trip, review with students that journals can document changes in events and feelings over time. Sometimes it is only in looking back over journals that we are able to gain perspective about important events. Because repeated observations are the focus of this activity, students will be conducting a walking field trip. The location will thus be one they can visit multiple times, regardless of financial constraints.

2. In preparation for the trip, explain that students will be selecting a particular location to journal about. It might be a busy storefront, a bus stop, a community garden, or a private residence. Their focus will be to record as much detail as possible during each visit. They will need to take note of elements that remain constant as well as things that change.

3. Arrange for multiple visits to the location, and during each visit support students in recording a detailed entry in their journal. Provide support as necessary to assist students in noticing small changes and details. Each student should observe a slightly different area of the location.

4. After multiple observations have been conducted, have students review all of their entries. Which day was particularly interesting to observe? Did they notice any patterns? What did they learn about the area? They should summarize their conclusions in a final entry.

5. After self-reflection, place students in groups of four and ask them to discuss their findings with their peers. Did they find any similar patterns with different locations or viewpoints?

6. As a culmination, students will be asked to select their favorite entry and share it with the class. They should read the entry aloud as well as share why they find this entry especially significant. Journals will then be collected and used as the final assessment piece.

Evaluation Rubric

	1	2	3
Nature Journal	Student records minimal information in the journal.	Journal entries are complete but some are brief, lacking detail.	Journal has a detailed entry for each day as well as a summary entry rich with description.

Modification

As with the activity for grade levels K–2, consider allowing English learners to incorporate their native language during the journaling process. A word bank will be helpful for these students as well.

Helpful Web Sites

These sites provide examples of nature journals that can be shared with students to prepare them for the activity.

American Museum of Natural History
http://www.amnh.org/nationalcenter/youngnaturalistawards/journal.html

New Horizons for Learning: Nature Journals
http://www.newhorizons.org/strategies/environmental/matsumoto.htm

ALSO CONSIDER . . .

Other field trip options to support learning in the language arts include

Newspaper/Magazine Editorial Offices: Students can learn about the many different tasks that go into creating a publication such as a newspaper or magazine, from copyediting to reporting. A nice postvisit activity would be to create a classroom newsletter with students taking on the different jobs they learned about during their field trip.

Retirement Community: Visiting a local retirement community provides an excellent opportunity for students to have stories read aloud to them as well as reading aloud to the residents. Pairing each student with a resident is one way to create a reading partnership. Older students can read to residents while younger students can enjoy a story read or shared orally.

Performances Based on Literature: Many communities have local theater groups that stage and produce plays based on popular children's stories. Check into reduced-price performances or even access to dress rehearsals. Back in the classroom, students can compare and contrast the work with the written version of the story as an exercise in critical analysis.

Professional Interview: To help students develop oral communication skills, arrange for a visit to a local business with enough employees for one-on-one interviews. Back in the classroom, students can put together formal presentations summarizing the data they collected.

Vignette: Author Investigation

"Oh my gosh . . . I can't believe she wrote this many books!"

"I couldn't even imagine writing one book . . . and she has like twenty!"

"Okay," Jennie said, trying to get her partners on task. "Our job is to do a quick survey of this author and her work. Who has the instruction sheet?"

"I do," said Kevin, as he smoothes out the slightly wrinkled paper.

"What do we do first?" asked Rashida.

"First we are supposed to record the title and date of publication of all the books located here in this library that our author wrote," Jennie answered.

"That's soooo many!" groaned Rashida.

(Continued)

(Continued)

"It's not if we split them between us," countered Kevin. Each student in the group grabbed a few of the books and began to record the publication data.

"How are we supposed to know if these are all the books she wrote?" said Jennie, partially to herself and partially to the group. The group was quiet as they thought about this challenge.

"Well," said Kevin, "this book has all her other books listed." The group looked at the list but soon realized that the book was published ten years earlier and did not include many of the more recent titles.

"I know!" shouted Rashida. There's a computer in the multimedia room of the library. We can do a search and try and find all of the books she wrote. She might even have her own Web site, she's so famous!"

Data Sheet 2 Author Investigation

Exploring Literature

Investigator:_____   Date:_____

Target Author:_____

How are these author's books similar?

_____

_____

_____

What are some key differences you notice?

_____

_____

_____

Identify the oldest book and the most recent book. Has the author's style changed much over time?

_____

_____

_____

How frequently does the author write a book? _____

Has he or she always worked with the same illustrator?   YES   NO

Why do you think this is the case?_____

_____

4

More Than Names and Dates

Social Science Explorations

Current reform efforts emphasize that the classroom social studies curriculum must move beyond simple instruction in names, dates, and events. Rather, it should focus on authentic, active learning opportunities involving reflection and decision making (National Council for the Social Studies, 1994). Many educators would agree that one successful way toward a quality social science curriculum is through interaction with primary sources, such as documents, historical objects, and authentic photographs (Chapin, 2005). But while these resources strongly support development of social science literacy on the part of our students, access to these items can be difficult for even the most resourceful educator. Field trip destinations can provide a wealth of opportunities for students to access these primary sources (Roberts, 1997; Sheilds, 1998) and may even be the only location where many students can engage with artifacts in a meaningful context.

STUDENTS AS ACTIVE RESEARCHERS: BRINGING THE SOCIAL SCIENCES ALIVE

Educators work hard to help students see the field of social studies not only as locations and dates but as a multifaceted area comprised of many different disciplines. Many who work in the social sciences are active researchers who rely on critical thinking and inquiry skills to help them solve the mysteries of the past as well to better understand society today. As we strive to teach students authentic ways of investigating issues in social science, tying to the work of professionals within the field is critical.

Researchers have for some time acknowledged the importance of active engagement on the part of students to support understanding as well as to increase motivation (e.g., Cooper, 2003; Hootstein, 1993; Thornton, 1997). National standards promote the opportunity for students to explore real-world issues and the work of social science researchers (National Council for the Social Studies, 1994). The most authentic way to explore the work of social science researchers is to take part in similar skills and processes. When students have access to informal social science learning institutions, these processes and experiences are given a more authentic context. Whereas in past decades a field trip was an opportunity for students to look and listen, a more current philosophy embraces the idea of students questioning, gathering data, and building conclusions.

Pace and Tesi (2004) studied adult memories of field trips and found that those who were actively engaged retained more information from their trip. Thus, as we create activities for our students that parallel the work of social studies professionals, the incorporation of active inquiry becomes imperative.

MAKING CONNECTIONS: INFORMAL LEARNING SITES AND THE SOCIAL SCIENCES

History Museums and Historic Homes

While students may joke about going back in time, the reality is that a visit to a historic home or history museum can provide that very opportunity. Clearly there are many different types of history museums and many different layouts of historic home facilities. Regardless of the layout, however, they all share one critical element: historic artifacts. The following activity will capitalize on this access to primary sources and authentic artifacts.

K–2ND GRADE ACTIVITY: I SPY!

One important tenet of social studies is for students to understand differences and similarities between objects of the past and objects of the present. This activity will help students make relevant connections between artifacts of the past and modern lifeways.

Objectives

- Students will observe historic artifacts and connect them to an object from today.
- Student will complete a "historian's journal" documenting their discoveries.

Curriculum Standards for Social Studies*
(National Council for the Social Studies, 1994)

- Theme 2: Time, Continuity, and Change
- Theme 3: People, Places, and Environments
- Theme 8: Science, Technology, and Society

Procedures

1. Before the field trip, identify the objects and artifacts that students will see during their visit. You can gather this information from online exhibition descriptions or by visiting the field trip site in advance. In the classroom, lead a discussion of objects students rely on every day. Do they drink from a glass? Does someone at home iron with an electric iron? Did they come to school in a car? Explain that during the field trip, students will see objects and artifacts that helped people with everyday tasks many years ago.

2. Before the trip, create activity sheets, combined into a "historian's journal" for students to complete during their visit. A sample data sheet that might be included in the historian's journal (Data Sheet 3) has been provided at the end of this chapter. Kindergarten students will most likely rely on simple pictures and key words. Second-grade students can be expected to use drawings and sentences. The activity sheets should begin with a picture of a common item from today. The rest of the activity sheet will ask students to identify an object at the museum or historic home that would have accomplished the same task years ago.

3. During the visit, assist students in completing their historian's journals. For example, if an activity sheet has a picture of a telephone, they will need to find something that was used for communication in the past, such as a desk set with a quill pen and ink. They will draw a picture of that discovery and describe how these two things were used in similar ways.

4. Back in the classroom, have students share their journals, first in cooperative groups and then in a class discussion of what items students discovered. Historian's journals will be collected and will serve as the evaluation piece for the activity.

Evaluation Rubric

	1	2	3
Historian's Journal	Little work is completed, and/or little effort shown.	There is some effort displayed and many sections of the journal have been completed.	Each section of the journal has been attempted at the highest level of effort.

Modification

Parent chaperones can assist with recording data by allowing younger students to dictate sentences. Students can also be placed in cooperative groups and complete one journal per group.

3RD–5TH GRADE ACTIVITY: NOW BUY THIS!

When faced with artifacts from the past, students can sometimes forget that there was a time when these items were new, significantly relied upon, and highly desired. This exercise will help students build that understanding.

Objectives

- Students will make observations of historic artifacts and reconstruct the context in which they were used.
- Students will complete a project outlining the use and purpose of an artifact in the format of an advertisement.

Curriculum Standards for Social Studies
(National Council for the Social Studies, 1994)

- Theme 2: Time, Continuity, and Change
- Theme 3: People, Places, and Environments
- Theme 7: Production, Distribution, and Consumption

Procedures

1. Before beginning the field trip, share advertisements from magazines with students. Discuss the objects or products being sold and what elements the companies focus on to attract a buyer. Next, display an object of any kind (pen, iron, paper clip, radio) and ask students to suggest information that would be important to include in an advertisement for this object as practice for the upcoming activity.

2. Before the trip, explain that while they are on the field trip they will see some historic artifacts that were equally important to someone's way of life during that time. They will be asked to select one artifact and take detailed notes on both the artifact and its usage. Back in the classroom, they will need to create a fictional advertisement from the time period of the artifact. The advertisement will need to celebrate the artifact's unique attributes, usage, and how the object would benefit the buyer.

3. During the field trip, provide students with clipboards and sketch paper. Bring along a digital camera to take photographs of the objects or artifacts that students decide to focus on. (*Note:* many museums do allow photography as long as the flash is disabled. Check with officials at the site to be sure.) These images can be incorporated into the advertisements. This activity can be completed in pairs or as individuals. Circulate among students to ensure they are recording enough information, and the kind of information that would be helpful in creating the final advertisement.

4. Back in the classroom, provide scratch paper for students to sketch out their advertisements. They should seek input from peers on this rough draft, adding information as necessary. For the final draft, provide a printed image of the object or artifact and high quality white construction paper to create the advertisement. Encourage the use of color and exciting language. Final advertisements will be collected and scored as the final assessment piece.

Evaluation Rubric

Advertisement	1	2	3
Content	Written portion is incorrect, not based on the field trip.	Written information is mostly accurate and based on the field trip, with some errors.	Written portion is well tied to information from the field trip, and is accurate.
Appearance	Advertisement shows little concern for neatness; work is hasty and sloppy.	Advertisement is nicely done; there are portions that could show more attention to detail and effort in the area of neatness.	Advertisement is neatly written and organized; presentation is excellent.

Extension

Students can create a second advertisement for a modern-day object with similar use. The two advertisements can be displayed next to each other on a course bulletin board or within a class book.

Helpful Web Sites

These sites provide information on historic homes and the types of artifacts one might find on display within.

Laura Ingalls Wilder Historic Home and Museum
http://www.lauraingallswilderhome.com

Rothchild House: Historic Home and Museum
http://www.jchsmuseum.org/Rothschild/house.html

Smithsonian Educational Resources
http://www.smithsonianeducation.org

Living History Experiences

Want to know what George Washington was thinking? Why not ask him? Think it was difficult to grind corn using a mortar and pestle? Try it yourself before making that decision. Living history experiences provide students with the opportunity to be immersed in a historical setting, surrounded by historical characters. Settings from colonial villages, pilgrim settlements, and military forts are just a few of the living history settings situated around the nation. The key element that separates a living history experience from a historic home for the purposes of this text is the presence of interpreters that have assumed the role of historical figures. Thus, the activities for this section will focus on interaction with that historical figure, though you may find that other activities within this chapter are equally applicable to a living history setting.

K–2ND GRADE ACTIVITY: TIME MACHINE TRAVEL

Younger students may find a living history experience so exciting it is overwhelming. It will be important to create enough structure so students can enjoy the experience while still providing enough freedom so they are not constrained by an overwhelming number of tasks.

Objectives

- Students will create a photo documentary of a living history experience.

Curriculum Standards for Social Studies
(National Council for the Social Studies, 1994)

- Theme 2: Time, Continuity, and Change
- Theme 3: People, Places, and Environments
- Theme 4: Individual Development and Identity

Procedures

1. Before beginning the activity, share magazines or informational texts with students to illustrate how photographs can help us visualize and understand the past. Explain that a powerful photograph needs only a small amount of text to tell a story.

2. Explain that students are going to take a field trip back in time and explain the historical context of the site selected for the visit. Inform students that they will act as reporters, taking pictures of what they see and adding description. How well they document this time period will be very important for when they "return to the present." They will be the only ones who can tell the story of this time and place.

3. Place students in groups and provide each group with a disposable camera. (*Note:* Digital cameras are also a wonderful option if your school has the resources and students are trained to use them.) Also provide an organizing sheet with space to record information for each picture that is taken. Each time a student clicks a frame, someone in the group can write a short phrase describing the context of the image. Teachers and parent chaperones can assist with this portion of the activity as necessary.

4. Back in the classroom, provide student groups with a large poster board and their developed prints. Students should use their notes to create a display—using the photos and simple sentences—documenting their "trip back in time." This project will serve as the final assessment piece.

Evaluation Rubric

	1	2	3
On-site Participation	Student is off task.	Student actively participates at times, but at other times is off task and not working with group.	Student is actively engaged in taking photographs and/or recording information.
Photo Project Participation	Student does not participate in poster creation or participates minimally.	Student provides some information for the poster project and assists in some arrangement of photos.	Student is actively engaged in creating the poster, adds information from the on-site experience, and makes decisions as to placement and arrangement of photographs.

Extension

With the help of parent chaperones, students can also use a digital video camera to document the visit, conducting mini-interviews of key historical characters.

3RD–5TH GRADE ACTIVITY: A DAY IN THE LIFE

One of the greatest benefits of sharing a living history experience with elementary students is the excitement of connecting with an actual person. Interviews are an excellent way to build on this opportunity and collect primary data. Interviewing an interpreter trained to stay in the character of a historical figure is a great way to help students understand history as a dynamic, relevant field of study.

Objectives

- Students will interview a historical figure regarding daily life in the nation's past.
- Students will create a class newsletter summarizing the information they discovered.

Curriculum Standards for Social Studies
(National Council for the Social Studies, 1994)

- Theme 2: Time, Continuity, and Change
- Theme 3: People, Places, and Environments
- Theme 4: Individual Development and Identity

Procedures

1. Before beginning the activity, check with the living history destination you have selected to ensure that conducting a short interview with the interpreters is possible. In addition, check on the option of recording any interview using a handheld tape recorder. This can facilitate data collection by students who struggle with literacy.

2. The main activity during the living history visit will be for students to conduct interviews in order to better understand lifeways of the past. Prepare students by sharing a video of a television interview or audio of a radio interview with someone historically significant to our time. Discuss the successful parts of the interview and the types of questions that were asked.

3. Explain to students that they will be exploring how life was during our nation's past by conducting their own interviews. As a class, decide on 10–20 interview questions they will use during their visit to the living history site. Then break these down so each group has between two and five different questions. Be sure to guide students toward open-ended questions to ensure they retrieve enough data for the activity. Also review polite protocol for beginning and ending an interview. Role playing among students can be helpful in teaching these techniques. Sample questions include the following:
   a. What chores do you do?
   b. How do you cook meals?
   c. What is your favorite thing to eat?
   d. Where do you go for school?
   e. What types of pets do you have?
   f. What do you do for fun?

4. During the visit, place students in preassigned groups and instruct them on the best way to connect with an interpreter for an interview. Some sites have interpreters walking around who will be happy to stop and chat. Others may have interpreters situated in particular locations, such as toiling in the fields or sewing in a parlor room.

5. Provide students with a way to record the interview, such as a handheld tape recorder. These can be purchased fairly inexpensively and will allow younger students to focus on the actual interview process rather than struggling with spelling and writing sentences that may be above their literacy level. During the visit, circulate among groups and take photos of the interview process. If recording is not possible, discuss a teamwork approach whereby one group member asks questions while another writes down responses.

6. Back in the classroom, either type up the dialogue from the tapes yourself or enlist the help of a parent or teaching assistant. With only a few questions per group, this should not take too much time. Questions can also be limited to one or two in line with availability of help in transcribing.

7. Once the data have been transcribed, provide each team with a copy of their questions and answers. Gather the students together as a class and prepare a large Venn diagram on butcher paper to record the results. A Venn diagram shows two intersecting circles that provide a graphic structure for comparing and contrasting topics.

8. As a class, encourage students to discuss what they discovered about lifeways of the past and compare it to their lifestyle today. Complete the Venn diagram as a class. Students will be evaluated on participation in both activities.

Evaluation Rubric

	No Credit	Credit
On-site Interview	Student is not an active participant in the on-site interview process.	Student actively participates in the on-site interview process, either asking questions or taking notes.
Class Discussion	Student does not participate in class discussion as either a contributor or an engaged listener.	Student actively participates in class discussion and completion of the Venn diagram.

Modification

Students who struggle with literacy can use pictures and also rely on the assistance of chaperones or peers with recording of information.

Helpful Web Sites

These Web sites will prepare students and educators for living history locations and related resources.

Colonial Williamsburg
http://history.org/history

Plimoth Plantation
http://www.plimoth.org

Wessels Living History Farm
http://www.livinghistoryfarm.org

Memorials, Monuments, and Historic Sites

Many historically significant locations are not building based. The location of a famous battle or early settlement may be marked only by a small plaque or sign. Some of these locations may have a larger monument commemorating a particular event, individual, or historic group. What these locations have in common is the need for significant preparation so the location can be fully understood and appreciated by students.

K–2ND GRADE ACTIVITY: REMEMBER THIS!

Students may pass by historic monuments or statues on a regular basis without considering the message behind the monument. This activity will help students understand a local monument as well as conceptualize a monument with personal relevance.

Objectives

- Students will visit a historic memorial or location and interpret its meaning.
- Students will design an original memorial with relevance to their local community.

Curriculum Standards for Social Studies
(National Council for the Social Studies, 1994)

- Theme 3: People, Places, and Environments
- Theme 5: Individuals, Groups, and Institutions

Procedures

1. Before the visit, share information with students about the type of monument, site, or memorial you will be visiting. If it is a statue, share images of other memorial statues. In preparation, share information about the site you will be visiting. If it is the site of a historic settlement or battle, share the background information, including any first-voice stories or journal entries that might be found through an Internet search.

2. During the visit, provide students with clipboards and plain, white paper. On the first sheet of paper, have them brainstorm any words, feelings, or images that come to mind when they view the site. For sites that may have looked different in the past (sites of historical events), encourage students to sketch on additional sheets what they feel the place might have looked like at the time of the event. Circulate among students to ensure that all have recorded information before returning to class.

3. Back in the classroom, lead a class discussion about students' sketches and writings. Were their thoughts captured in whatever plaque or statue was present? Is there a need for more information to convey the important messages of the site? Review how simple plaques, statues, or monuments need to convey a large message, and the potential difficulty in designing this successfully.

4. Explain that students will be creating a monument or memorial to honor an important event in their own family or community. Review how simple images can symbolize large ideas and identify the types of events that are important to remember years later. Some students will make choices such as a bronze tooth to commemorate a first lost tooth. Others may select memorials with broader or darker themes, such as plaque near the site of an accident or fire. As this activity focuses on events "historically significant" to students, it is critical to validate all responses and selections.

5. Ask students to design a monument or memorial or draft text for a plaque centered on this selected event. It will be helpful to provide a range of images from plaques and memorials around the nation so students are aware of the scope the project can take. Once the task is completed, ask students to share their image or text in a class discussion. Student designs will be collected and used as the final assessment piece.

Evaluation Rubric

	No Credit	Credit
Memorial/Monument Design	Student did not create a monument or memorial design in line with class discussion.	Student made significant effort to create an original design of a monument or memorial as outlined by the instructor.

Extension

If students select an event or occurrence with significant community impact, it may be appropriate to share the work with local officials. It may even lead to a permanent marker within the community.

3RD–5TH GRADE ACTIVITY: WE'RE IN CHARGE NOW

This activity builds on the the memorial/monument activity for Grades K–2, yet asks older students to think on a larger and perhaps even controversial scale. They will be asked to design a memorial for a significant historical event in line with the grade-level curriculum (see the vignette at the end of this chapter).

Objectives

- Students will critically analyze the design of a nationally significant memorial or monument.
- Students will select a significant event in history (war, civic demonstration, natural disaster, etc.) and design a monument or memorial to honor the event.

Curriculum Standards for Social Studies
(National Council for the Social Studies, 1994)

- Theme 1: Culture
- Theme 2: Time, Continuity, and Change
- Theme 3: People, Places, and Environments
- Theme 10: Civic Ideals and Practices

Procedures

1. Before the visit, discuss the role of historic memorials or monuments in preserving and honoring the past. Discuss memorials that students might be familiar with, using images from books or the Internet to support the discussion.

2. Explain that students will be in charge of designing a memorial as a class assignment. It is best to pick one event for all students to focus on and to select one in line with the curriculum. For example, if students are studying the Oregon Trail, they may be asked to design a memorial for the tragedy that befell the Donner Party. Explain that students will be visiting a local memorial as research for designing an original memorial.

3. During the visit, place students in groups and provide them with clipboards and open-ended activity sheets to help guide their analysis of the site. Questions might include the following:
   a. How does the structure of the monument or memorial relate to the event?
   b. How does the site make you feel?
   c. Does the site provide necessary content information about the event?
   d. Does the site honor all individuals that were affected by the event?
   e. What would make this memorial or monument even more effective?

4. Back in the classroom, lead a class discussion on the memorial observed during the field trip. Encourage students to share their thoughts and the notes they recorded. Ask groups of students to design a detailed memorial or monument in line with the assigned historic event. Provide significant time for students to make detailed sketches, provide measurements, draft any label text, and create a quality "proposal."

5. As a final step, students can present their proposals to another class at the same grade level and let students vote on which one they would build if they had the resources. This is in line with how many memorial designs are finalized. Proposals will be collected and serve as the final assessment piece alongside student participation at the field trip site.

Evaluation Rubric

	1	2	3
On-site Participation	Student is off task.	At times student actively participates in cooperative groups, but at other times is off task and not working with the group.	Student is actively engaged in cooperative group work and note taking during the field trip.
Final Proposal	Student does not participate in creation of the group design proposal and associated presentation.	Student contributes to the group design proposal, but at times is off task or not engaged with the group during proposal creation and/or associated presentation.	Student is actively engaged in cooperative group activity, contributing significantly to the design proposal and associated presentation.

Extension

Remind students of opportunities in architecture and design as a career. Maya Lin, designer of the Vietnam War Memorial, was selected after winning a design contest while still in college. Her youth, her Chinese American background, and her nontraditional design ideas all broke new ground and can serve as an inspiration to students.

Helpful Web Sites

These sites will provide information on historic locations, memorials, and monuments to guide a field trip or to explore an area outside your community.

National Park Service
http://www.cr.nps.gov

United States Senate: Monuments and Memorials
http://www.senate.gov/pagelayout/visiting/one_item_and_teasers/monuments_img_coll.htm

Cemeteries

Cemeteries are wonderful field trip destinations for learning about a town's past. Careful investigation of names, dates, and gravestone groupings can provide insight into when a town was founded, times of significant illnesses or disasters, and family lineage. A smaller community cemetery may prove a more authentic visit site than a large, modern cemetery, which may not honor or include the entire history of a town.

Visits to cemeteries will take a little special planning. First, it is important to contact the groundskeeper or facility manager and discuss plans for a visit. It will be critical to assure him or her that students will be respectful and that the visit is a serious part of a school project. Second, prepare students and their families for the trip by sending a written notice home explaining plans for the visit. It is important to emphasize that the trip is part of a historical case study, not a "ghost hunting" adventure. In addition, it is a good idea to leave a copy of the lesson plan with the school principal or headmaster in case a concerned parent or community member makes contact with the school. This way, the details of your activity are sure to be conveyed correctly. Last, take into account any special circumstances on the part of students. For example, it may be best to reschedule a cemetery visit to the following year if a young student has recently lost a sibling or parent.

K–2ND GRADE ACTIVITY: OUR TOWN

Exploring a cemetery with our youngest students will take some special planning and preparation. Explain to students that they are going to pretend they are historians from a different state. They will be exploring the local cemetery to learn a little more about the history of their town.

Objectives

- Students will explore gravestones and monuments within a local cemetery.
- Students will record the data they discover in specialized historian's journals.

Curriculum Standards for Social Studies
(National Council for the Social Studies, 1994)

- Theme 2: Time, Continuity, and Change
- Theme 3: People, Places, and Environments

Procedures

1. Prepare for the visit by brainstorming with students the types of things they might be able to learn about a town by exploring a local cemetery. For example, students can make estimates as to the age of a town by identifying the oldest gravestone. Older markers may be of a different type of stone than newer markers. Students may notice that certain types of engravings or statuary are common during different decades. This preliminary discussion may take more scaffolding with

younger students than with older students. You may find a discussion of fictional cemetery stories (ghosts and vampires) necessary to address student concerns and prepare them for the reality of the trip.

2. Before the visit, create an open-ended historian's journal in which students can record their discoveries. Each page of the log should correspond to elements already discussed and allow for students to record information they find personally interesting. Chaperones can help preliterate students interpret the directions on each page and complete the log. Sample investigation questions might include the following:
   a. What is the oldest gravestone you can find?
   b. Draw one of the pictures you saw on a marker. What do you think it means?
   c. What dates are the most common? 1700s? 1800s? 1900s?
   d. What last names do you see more than once?
   e. Draw an old marker. Draw a new marker. How are they the same? How are they different?

3. Before leaving the site, find a place to sit as a group. Encourage students to share their discoveries and lead a discussion of what these discoveries tell us about the history of the area. For example, a cemetery with gravestones no older than the early 1900s indicates a young town. If one family's name appears over and over, it could indicate an important or founding family.

4. Once back in the classroom, cut and paste from students' historian's journal to create a class book of the data collected. Be sure to include a conclusion page at the end to sum up what students discovered. It might be nice to create a newsletter outlining student discoveries to send home to parents. Perhaps the governing body of the cemetery might also be interested in a copy! The student historian's journal will be used as the final assessment piece.

Evaluation Rubric

	1	2	3
Historian's Journal	Only a few sections are competed, with little detail and effort.	The majority of sections are completed with significant effort. -OR- All sections are completed with some effort and detail.	Each section is completed with the student's best effort.

Modifications

Younger students who are still developing their reading/writing skills can use pictures to capture their discoveries, or parent chaperones can record student-generated sentences for them. Crayons and white paper can also be used to create rubbings of newer markers, rather than students needing to copy down inscriptions. For conservation reasons, rubbings of older, crumbling markers should be avoided. For kindergarten students, it may be best to conduct the investigation as a whole group with teacher scaffolding.

3RD–5TH GRADE ACTIVITY: OUR TOWN

Like the version for younger students, this activity asks students to gather data from information on gravestones in order to draw conclusions about a town's history.

Objectives

- Students will explore gravestones and monuments within a local cemetery.
- Students will record the data relating to a self-selected research question.

Curriculum Standards for Social Studies
(National Council for the Social Studies, 1994)

- Theme 1: Culture
- Theme 2: Time, Continuity, and Change
- Theme 3: People, Places, and Environments

Procedures

1. Before the visit, discuss the work of social scientists with students. Begin by explaining that social scientists will form a question or select a general content area they would like to know more about. Explain to students that they will be conducting their own research study around a question of their choice.

2. Begin explaining that students will form an area of study that interests them related to their neighborhood cemetery. Sample questions might include the following:
   a. Can I find my family name there? How many times?
   b. What do older gravestones look like?
   c. Are there any special gravestones for soldiers?
   d. Are there any gravestones that celebrate a foreign culture?

3. During the visit, provide students with clipboards, pencils, and blank paper. Help guide investigations by writing the student's question at the top of the first piece of blank paper. As they move through the cemetery, circulate to ensure that students are recording data related to their questions. Some may be able to get right to work. Others may need more structure and may benefit from working in a cooperative group.

4. Back in the classroom, provide students with poster boards to create a presentation of their data. Provide a variety of paper, pens, and art materials to help create a visually interesting project. Help them create a layout that clearly accentuates their investigation question as well as the information that was collected. If a thank-you note is sent to the contact person at the cemetery, it might be nice to include images and details of the final projects to demonstrate how valuable the visit was. The final project will serve as the scored assessment piece.

Evaluation Rubric

Final Project	1	2	3
Project Content	Project is not tied to field trip; data presented are not tied to the student's research question.	Project is somewhat linked to the field trip; data are somewhat related to the student's	Project is well focused; data are presented clearly and support student's area of

Final Project	1	2	3
		question, but overall the project is not cohesive; more research is needed.	inquiry; there is an explicit tie to the field trip.
Neatness/ Organization	Student's project shows little effort in the area of neatness and organization.	Student's project demonstrates some advanced planning and effort in the area of neatness and organization.	Student's final project is neat, well planned, and demonstrates a high degree of organization and care.

Modification

If students are not prepared to work independently, they can be placed in pairs or small groups for the research project.

Helpful Web Sites

Arlington National Cemetery

This site serves as an excellent resource on the monuments of Arlington as well as the role the cemetery plays in the history of the United States.
http://www.arlingtoncemetery.org

Association for Gravestone Studies

This association promotes the preservation of gravestones as well as their role in historical studies.
http://www.gravestonestudies.org

Cemetery Transcription Network

This site provides general information about cemeteries and grave markers as well as a search engine to explore specific details about cemeteries around the world.
http://www.interment.net

Note: Many online resources for cemetery studies are state specific. A simple search will easily provide several Web sites specific to your geographic region.

SPECIAL CONSIDERATION: CULTURAL DESTINATIONS

Many of the activities above are specific to field trip destinations with a historic focus. However, social science also covers a wealth of topics specific to cultural diversity. There are a number of field trip destinations, from museums to monuments, that support public understanding of different cultures and lifeways. These are wonderfully rich field trip destinations and should be made a part of the curriculum whenever possible. Because many of these sites explore different cultures through a historic or artistic lens, several of the activities in this book will be excellent matches for these field trips.

Specific activities on cultural interpretation as a field trip activity were not designed for inclusion in this work for several reasons. Primarily, how these sites encourage students to engage with the content and emotion of the complex experiences of a different culture will vary greatly from site to site. Some sites may encourage students to take on the perspective of another individual through role play and empathetic dialogue. Others may find a more respectful approach is for students to have the benefit of hearing directly from representative members of a particular community without trying to assume the role of anyone other than themselves.

I would encourage you to consult with the cultural institution you plan to visit about what types of activities they feel would best allow students to gain understanding and insight in the most appropriate and respectful way, in line with the exhibition philosophy of the site. Taking the lead from the professionals of these particular institutions is sure to result in a successful visit.

ALSO CONSIDER . . .

Other field trip options to support social science learning include

Natural History Museums: Some equate natural history museums only with science, but these institutions often house exhibits and research departments in the area of human culture and history. The activities conducted at a history museum may be equally relevant here.

Historic or Culturally Influenced Neighborhood: Many communities have areas where historic buildings or neighborhoods celebrate and honor a particular culture. These visits can help students better understand the rich offerings of their own communities in line with social studies curricular goals.

Specialty Food Store: When learning about different cultures, trying or simply learning about new foods is an exciting way for students to broaden their horizons. Arranging a visit to a specialty food store, with some discussion led by a store employee, is one way to share this information with students.

Retirement Community: One place to practice collecting oral histories is at a local retirement community or assisted-living facility. It will be important to arrange permission well ahead of time and determine which residents are most willing to work with students. Not only is this a great learning opportunity for students, it will most likely be a welcome treat for residents to be able to share their most precious memories with a new generation.

Vignette: Student Designers

"Remember, it's critical that we stay together. There are a lot of visitors here today and we don't want to lose anyone!" Mr. Edwards cautioned his fifth graders as they made their way to their second stop: the Korean War Veterans Memorial.

Students immediately broke into preassigned pairs and began taking notes and making sketches on their clipboards. Natalie whispered to her partner, "I really like how there are people in the background of the wall. . . . It's kinda like they're not the center . . . but just as important."

Kanye nodded and continued to sketch the general layout of the monument. "It's so spread out," he commented as he turned in a slow circle, "not like the Vietnam Veterans Memorial Wall we just saw."

"How come there aren't any names?! I think it's important to put all the names," Emi said to the teacher.

"You don't need names to have a monument. It's kinda like one big 'thank you' to the soldiers," Trevon countered.

"How come this monument is so much bigger than the Vietnam Veterans Memorial? This one is so much fancier!" Karen asked Mr. Edwards with genuine confusion.

"Because lots of people didn't agree with the Vietnam War. That's what my grandpa said," Terrence answered with considerable fifth-grade authority.

"Hmmm . . . how could this discussion relate to the monument we will be designing?" Mr. Edwards cautioned before moving to the next group. He tried to remain as silent as possible as he walked among the students, leaving them to raise the difficult issues and discussion points. He was pleased to hear students addressing issues of controversy and disagreement.

After twenty minutes, Mr. Edwards clapped his hands and gathered the students around him once more. He made sure to check that all students had recorded something on their clipboards. This data would be critical for their follow-up project of designing a fictional memorial for the Civil War.

Data Sheet 3 Artifact Investigation

Now and Then

Historian:_____   Date:_____

Location:_____

Now we use . . .	In the past people used . . .
Telephone	
Electric Lamp	
Microwave	

5

One, Two, Three, Go!

Math Explorations

Developing student proficiency in mathematics is at the heart of current reform efforts (Burch & Spillane, 2003). But being mathematically literate means more than simply succeeding academically within the K–12 setting. The National Research Council (1999) also points out the importance of being able to apply mathematical knowledge to everyday situations and authentic contexts, much like the work of actual mathematicians. Thus these reform efforts call for students to connect mathematical concepts to their daily lives and situations from the natural and social sciences, medicine, and commerce (National Council of Teachers of Mathematics, 1991). Field trips are one way to provide students with the opportunity to experience problem solving within an authentic context, as well as explore integrated math experiences. Not only does this context support the development of content understanding (Ladson-Billings, 1995), a math-focused field trip can result in added engagement on the part of students (Rosenthal & Ampadu, 1999), promoting more positive feelings toward math studies.

BEYOND BASICS

Recent reform efforts have worked to change student (and parent) perceptions of math as strictly computation and basic skills. While mastery of basic skills is critical, equally significant is the opportunity to apply basic computation skills to more authentic, real-world problem solving. In fact, this rich exposure to mathematical engagement can help students achieve higher levels of competency than previously thought (Greenes, Ginsburg, & Balfanz, 2004). Problem-based math experiences can also support students in generating a more positive attitude toward mathematics (Weber-Russell & LeBlanc, 2004). In addition, mathematics taught within a problem-based, authentic context provides support in the development of other curricular areas such as language arts and literacy (Greenes, Ginsburg, & Balfanz, 2004). Researchers further assert the importance of math being presented to students within the context of real-world applications in order to successful meet the needs of a diverse student body (Croom, 1997). This approach reaffirms the belief that success in mathematics is possible for all students when authentic context is applied.

MAKING CONNECTIONS: INFORMAL LEARNING SITES AND MATHEMATICS

Grocery Store

A class field trip to a local grocery store can provide students with a wealth of opportunities to explore mathematics in an authentic context. From fractions in the produce aisle to making change at the checkout counter, the local market is indeed a learning lab of problem solving.

Different stores will have different regulations and procedures regarding school visits. When preparing for a market field trip, be sure to contact the store management well in advance regarding your plans. Most national chains require prior arrangements to be made with the store manager before your class can be granted access. At this time, discuss the different ideas you have in mind for activities. Some local stores might be open to students taking items off shelves, while others may want an "observation only" visit. Last, many national chains do not allow photography without special permission. If you would like to photograph your students at work, be sure to make arrangements for this well in advance.

K–2ND GRADE ACTIVITY: HOW MUCH IS A POUND?

This activity provides an opportunity for students to weigh different vegetables and fruits and gain practice using a scale as well as build understanding on just how much a pound is. Students can also practice estimation skills during the investigation. Because this activity will involve handling of produce without purchase, check with the manager ahead of time.

Objectives

- Students will weigh different fruits and vegetables to determine how many of each total one pound.
- Students will make estimates based on earlier calculations.

Principles and Standards for School Mathematics*
(National Council of Teachers of Mathematics, 2000)

- Standard 4: Measurement
- Standard 5: Data Analysis and Probability
- Standard 7: Reasoning and Proof

*Source: Reprinted with permission from the *Principles and Standards for School Mathematics,* © copyright 2000 by the National Council of Teachers of Mathematics. Standards are listed with the permission of the National Council of Teachers of Mathematics (NCTM). NCTM does not endorse the content or validity of these alignments.

Procedures

1. Before the visit, share flyers from local markets with students. Identify the different examples of fruits and vegetables for sale by the pound. Highlight that $3.99 for a whole pound may sound like a bargain, but ask students if they know exactly how many apples (or oranges, or cucumbers) make up a single pound.

2. In preparation for the visit, create a "grocery journal" for students, with images of common fruits and vegetables together with a place for students to record how many they will get of each if they purchase one pound. On the last page, provide space for an additional estimation activity based on the data students have collected from the actual weighing of produce. Select a fruit or vegetable similar in size and shape to an item students have already weighed. Ask students to estimate how many of this item would make up one pound based on what they have already learned. Providing practice with scales in the classroom will help students feel more comfortable with using the scales in the grocery store.

3. During the trip, place students in cooperative groups with an adult chaperone to assist each group. Have students move through the produce section, weighing fruits and vegetables listed in their journals to determine how many are required to make up a single pound. Students should record outcomes in their grocery journals.

4. For the last question, ask students to work with their groups to calculate an estimate. Estimates should be based on the data already collected by comparing known weights with the type of fruit or vegetable at the focus of the estimation. Before leaving the store, gather all students together and do a demonstration to determine the correct answer, by actually weighing the designated fruits or vegetables. Ask students to write the actual number next to their estimate.

5. Back in the classroom, discuss overall findings. Were students surprised to see how many (or how few) fruits or vegetables made up a pound? How did they decide on their estimate? What other fruit or vegetable did they use to help them guess? How close was their estimate to the correct response?

6. Revisit the grocery flyers that began the discussion. Do students still feel the advertised prices are a bargain?

Evaluation Rubric

	No Credit	Credit
Completion of Grocery Journal	Very little or none of the grocery journal completed.	All or nearly all of the grocery journal completed.

Extension

Students can extend the concept of estimating size or weight to other situations. A second trip to the grocery store can focus on the net weight of packaged items or pasta and grains.

3RD–5TH GRADE ACTIVITY: UNDER BUDGET

Concepts in money and making change can be challenging for students, even with the help of manipulatives. In this activity, students practice estimation skills as well as adding monetary amounts and calculating change.

Objectives

- Students select items for "purchase" within a set budget.
- Students calculate a final total and identify the amount of change they will receive.

Principles and Standards for School Mathematics*
(National Council of Teachers of Mathematics, 2000)

- Standard 1: Number and Operations
- Standard 6: Problem Solving
- Standard 9: Connections

Procedures

1. Before the visit, address the importance of making estimations in everyday situations. We may estimate how much food to buy or estimate how much groceries will cost before we get to the checkout counter. Estimation is important when doing precise calculations will take too much time or may not be possible.

2. In preparation for the visit, inform students that they will be placed in cooperative groups and provided with a budget to buy food for an imaginary occasion. One example might be a budget of $10 to prepare a recess snack for the class. Before the visit, it will be important to build skills in adding and subtracting monetary amounts. This way the visit can reinforce skills, rather than create a novel situation that might make acquisition of a new skill even more difficult.

3. During the visit, place students in cooperative groups with a parent chaperone. Provide each group with a clipboard and an open-ended activity sheet for students to list the items they would like to purchase and to keep a running estimation record. Students will gather their groceries in a handheld basket, completing their activity sheet as they go. (Work with the market manager to determine what the parameters for this activity should be. For example, allowing students to handle only nonperishable items such as canned soup or cake mix may be one restriction you place on the activity.) This can be accomplished by using estimation and rounding skills learned earlier in class. The goal will be to get as close to their budgeted amount without going over. (*Note:* If you live in a state that has sales tax, you will need to add instruction on how to estimate your state tax, as well as the items to which it applies.) If actual gathering of groceries is not permitted without purchase, see the modification section of this lesson plan for alternatives.

4. After they have completed "shopping," students will present their groceries for a final total check. You'll need to check ahead of time with the market manager to determine what the best way to conduct the activity would be. A community-friendly market might allow use of an actual checkout counter if your visit is during quiet hours. Others might request that a parent chaperone use a calculator and a hand-held price scanner out of the way of busy shoppers. A third option is to have the parent chaperone use a calculator to tally prices as students remove items from the marked shelves, sharing the grand total at the end of the visit.

*Standards are listed with the permission of the National Council of Teachers of Mathematics (NCTM). NCTM does not endorse the content or validity of these alignments.

5. Before leaving the market, identify the group that came closest to using their full budget without going over. A simple award certificate can be prepared to recognize their "Excellent Estimation" or "Bountiful Budgeting" success. A last step to complete on site will be for students to work together to reshelve any groceries collected that are not being purchased.

6. Back in the classroom, hold a class discussion to debrief students on the activity. Were there any surprises? What was the most difficult aspect of the activity? Students will turn in their budget activity sheets as the final assessment piece.

Evaluation Rubric

	1	2	3
Budgeting Activity	Activity sheet meets 1 of 3 criteria: • detailed list of groceries; • running estimation; • actual total compared to budgeted amount.	Activity sheet meets 2 of the 3 criteria.	Activity sheet meets all 3 criteria.

Modification

Some grocery stores may not want students to take items they are not planning to purchase from the shelves, even temporarily. Others might allow the handling of nonperishables, but prefer that milk, eggs, or frozen foods not be carried around only to be reshelved. If that is the case, the activity can be conducted in the same way, but with the parent chaperone keeping an official record of each item students would have placed in their shopping basket, and the exact price as listed on the shelf. Contacting the store manager well in advance will be the best way to ensure the activity you design will work with any health restrictions the market may impose.

Extension

If it is possible to secure funding, either through parent donations or a small grant, the group who came closest to their limit without going over can be allowed to purchase the groceries and move forward with the event plan.

Helpful Web Sites

Maryland Public Television: Dollars and Sense
This site designed for children will allow them to explore the process of earning, spending, and saving money.
http://senseanddollars.thinkport.org

U.S. Food and Drug Administration: Center for Food Safety and Applied Nutrition
This site provides overview information on how to read and interpret nutritional labels on food.
http://www.cfsan.fda.gov/~dms/foodlab.html

Home Improvement Store

A home improvement or hardware store is an excellent place for students to explore authentic applications of measurement and geometry. Deciding how much paint to buy is directly linked to lessons in area. Purchasing fencing is rooted in accurate calculations of perimeter. The concept of volume is demonstrated in a square planter and the amount of cubic soil to fill it. In fact, it is likely that a single visit will not be enough to accomplish all the possible learning activities.

K–2ND GRADE ACTIVITY: BUY THAT FENCE!

Providing opportunities for students to apply mathematical problem solving to real-world situations is critical to developing math skills that go beyond basic computation. This activity draws connections between geometry, measurement, and a simple trip to the hardware store.

Objectives

- Students will select the type of fencing best suited for an area of the playground
- Students will calculate the perimeter of an area on the playground to be fenced (second grade only).
- Students will calculate how much different fencing options will cost based on this perimeter (second grade only).

Principles and Standards for School Mathematics*
(National Council of Teachers of Mathematics, 2000)

- Standard 1: Number and Operation
- Standard 3: Geometry
- Standard 4: Measurement
- Standard 6: Problem Solving

Procedures

1. Before the visit, students will work with the teacher to identify an area of the schoolyard that could benefit from a fence. This might be a class garden space or perhaps a play area designated for younger students. It will be important to explain to students they will not really be installing a fence, but that they will be practicing their math skills on a real-world problem.

2. In preparation for the visit, students will work with the teacher to understand that they will need to buy enough fencing to enclose the whole area. Younger students (Grades K–1) will work with the teacher to measure the amount needed directly by using a measuring tape or other age-appropriate method. Students in second grade can be introduced to the term *perimeter* and do some practice calculations.

---

*Standards are listed with the permission of the National Council of Teachers of Mathematics (NCTM). NCTM does not endorse the content or validity of these alignments.

3. During the field trip visit, the class will work as a whole to explore the different fencing options. Encourage creativity relating to the function of the space. The option of a simple brick perimeter may be best for a garden project, but a higher fence may be necessary to separate a portion of the schoolyard.

4. With store permission, take digital photographs of the different options and have a parent chaperone or student record the price for each. Some stores might have take-away images or even fencing samples. Older students may be given their own "measurement journals" to record data, while younger students will be most successful conducting the investigation as a whole group with teacher mediation. This is a time to address broad mathematical issues. For example, price differences may not seem that large when looking at the per foot price. However, when you multiply that by the amount needed, perhaps as much as 50 feet, a price difference of $2 per foot can become very large. The teacher can ask students to reflect on these issues and come up with some solutions.

5. Back in the classroom, lead a class discussion of the different fencing options. Ask students to indicate which one they prefer and then place students in cooperative groups based on this preference. Give each group a poster board where they can display the name and image of the type of fencing.

6. Depending on students' mathematical skills, they can also present the amount of fencing needed, using diagrams as appropriate. They may also choose to calculate the total cost of the fence using a calculator. These final poster boards, and student engagement in their creation, will be assessed.

Evaluation Rubric

	1	2	3
Project Participation	Student is not actively engaged.	Student is partially engaged at different stages of the project.	Student is actively engaged at all stages of the project.
Final Project	Final project contains 1 or none of 3 components: <ul><li>image/ description of fencing;</li><li>correct perimeter calculations (as age appropriate);</li><li>correct pricing calculations (as age appropriate).</li></ul>	Final project contains 2 of the 3 components.	Final project contains all 3 components.

Extensions

Additional measurement tasks can be incorporated into a single trip. Students may want to calculate the amount of tile needed for the classroom or paint needed for the walls, the size of a rug for story time, or the number of benches for seating in a school garden.

3RD–5TH GRADE ACTIVITY: FILL THOSE POTS

Students love to garden. It could be they enjoy digging in dirt, or perhaps it is the reward of watching a carefully tended plant bloom. This activity addresses the math behind gardening, utilizing concepts in measurement and geometry as a guide.

Objectives

- Students will calculate the volume of a variety of different pots.
- Students will use this data to determine how much soil to purchase.

Principles and Standards for School Mathematics*
(National Council of Teachers of Mathematics, 2000)

- Standard 1: Number and Operation
- Standard 3: Geometry
- Standard 4: Measurement
- Standard 6: Problem Solving

Procedures

1. Before the visit, students should review the process for calculating the volume of three-dimensional shapes that are commonly used for planters: for example, rectangular solid (L × W × H), cube (L × W × H), and cylinder (3.14 r^2h).

2. In preparation for the visit, provide each student with an activity sheet or sheets with space to make between three and six calculations, depending on time available. Each space should provide room to sketch the planter and label sides with the appropriate measurement, as well as an area to do calculations. There should also be space to record the size of three different bags of soil. Back in the classroom, students will need to decide how much soil they will have to buy in order to fill all the pots. A place to record this grand total of soil needed also needs to be included on the activity sheet(s).

3. During the visit, place students in pairs to complete their activity sheets. Provide each group with a flexible measuring tape, clipboards, activity sheets, pencils, and calculators to check their computation. It will be helpful to include the formulas for key shapes on the activity sheets.

4. Lead students to the display of different planters and encourage them to spread out so they have room to work. Also, provide assistance as necessary to reach planters placed on high shelves, or planters too heavy for students to move. During the activity, circulate as necessary to support students' computation.

5. As students work, they may notice that many planters are not a perfect cylinder. Remind them they are doing these calculations to estimate how much soil is needed to fill the pot. If a planter is not a perfect cylinder, the students can do the calculations for a perfect cylinder and then make a note that the actual volume may be less because the planter bottom is slightly narrower than the top.

6. After students have made planter calculations, they will need to move to the soil aisle. There, students will need to record how much soil comes in a bag, providing data for three different sizes. Remind students that in science and math it is important to always use metric units.

7. Back in the classroom, students will work in groups of six to share their calculations and determine how much soil each pair of students will need to purchase.

---

*Standards are listed with the permission of the National Council of Teachers of Mathematics (NCTM). NCTM does not endorse the content or validity of these alignments.

Students will record this figure on the final space of their activity sheet(s). Students will turn in completed activity sheets as a final assessment piece.

Evaluation Rubric

Final Project	1	2	3
On-site Participation (individual score)	Student is not actively engaged.	Student is partially engaged at different stages of the investigation.	Student is actively engaged at all stages of the investigation.
Final Project (group score)	Activity sheet contains 1 or none of 3 components: • correct volume calculations; • soil data; • final total of soil needed for planting.	Activity sheet contains 2 of the 3 components.	Activity sheet contains all 3 components with supporting data.

Modification

One benefit of field trips is that students are often able to tackle concepts that in a traditional classroom may prove too difficult. The unique setting can often inspire students to really stretch their abilities. Volume calculations are not a concept regularly tackled by third- and fourth-grade students within the classroom curriculum. However, it is not uncommon to see students tackling complex calculations when immersed in a real-world setting. So while of course this activity can easily be modified to include fewer calculations and focus instead on more conceptual aspects of estimation as deemed appropriate by the classroom teacher, appropriate cooperative grouping and effective teacher scaffolding may be the only modification necessary to ensure success.

Extension

Finances permitting, this planning activity could be a single step in the process to creating a "container garden" at the school site. Student calculations could translate into an actual potting project. If finances at the school site are limited, explore possible partnerships with a local nursery, which may be willing to donate plants or related planting material.

Helpful Web Sites

Most home improvement stores have an associated Web site that may contain helpful items such as calculation programs to determine the amount of carpeting needed to cover a particular room or tips on measuring fencing. The most effective Web site will be the one that corresponds to the specific business you choose to visit.

Zoos

The connection between zoos and the life sciences is clear. However, much of scientific study is rooted strongly in math and statistics. A zoo or other animal sanctuary is a dynamic location to launch studies in quantitative data gathering, from percentages of species to timed observations. While planning a zoo investigation, it will be important to take into account the size of the space and plan for rest breaks for younger students. In addition, a hot day may prompt many animals to retire from sight. Trips planned for the cooler months may result in more active animal subjects.

K–2ND GRADE ACTIVITY: HOW MANY OF EACH?

Zoos boast a large variety of animals from many different classes or groups. In this activity, students collect data on the different animals they encounter and create a chart identifying the percentage of animals from each class.

Objectives

- Students sort zoo animals into different groups.
- Students tally the number of animals within each group and convert to percentages using calculators.
- Students create a bar graph summarizing their results.

Principles and Standards for School Mathematics*
(National Council of Teachers of Mathematics, 2000)

- Standard 5: Data Analysis and Probability
- Standard 6: Problem Solving
- Standard 9: Connections

Procedures

1. Before the visit, review with students that there are many different ways to group animals. We can group them by where they live, what they eat, or how they raise their young. How you decide to group animals will depend on the types of animals that your particular zoo houses. One option is group animals into five classes: mammals, birds, reptiles, amphibians, and fish. (*Note:* Although there are seven classes in total, this five-class grouping is a simple way to learn classification.) Briefly review each class to facilitate data gathering at the site.

2. In preparation for the visit, prepare an activity sheet with a square for each class of animal. Students will record the names of each animal they see within the appropriate box. A sample data sheet has been provided at the end of this chapter (Data Sheet 4).

3. During the visit, place students in cooperative groups and provide each group with a clipboard and data sheet. Inform students that they will take turns recording data throughout the visit. Parent chaperones can assist with recording of data as necessary, as well as help students to classify animals correctly. By the end of the visit, each box should have a list of animals as well as a grand total of the number of animals within each class.

4. If the zoo is too large to cover comfortably in one day, an alternative to each group covering the whole space is to assign specific areas of the zoo to each cooperative group. Groups may still visit unassigned areas to enjoy the exhibits, but they will be responsible for recording data only in conjunction with their assigned site.

---

*Standards are listed with the permission of the National Council of Teachers of Mathematics (NCTM). NCTM does not endorse the content or validity of these alignments.

5. Back in the classroom, assist students with constructing a bar graph summarizing their data. Providing a guiding structure as seen on Data Sheet 4 will be helpful for students.

6. A class discussion should follow the presentations, addressing any discrepancies between findings and possible explanations for these differences. For example, some students may have missed an exhibit and thus not included it in their tally. Data collected from different areas can be synthesized as a class.

7. Completed activity sheets (inclusive of the bar graph) and oral presentations will be the final assessment piece.

Evaluation Rubric

Final Project	1	2	3
On-site Data Gathering	Student is not actively engaged.	Student is partially engaged, at times working with group but at other times off task.	Student is an active group participant, counting animals and recording data.
Data Analysis and Presentation	Student does not demonstrate active engagement.	Student participates in both bar graph creation and the oral presentation with some engagement.	Student actively engages in bar graph creation as well as the oral presentation.

Modifications

Younger students may need more scaffolding during the creation of the bar graph. An alternative to creating the chart from scratch would be to provide students with a half-completed or completely outlined graph that simply requires coloring and labeling. Another alternative is to utilize student-centered graphing software programs to create a computer-generated graph based on data the students input.

3RD–5TH GRADE ACTIVITY: WHAT ARE THEY DOING?

Many animal researchers spend a lot of time recording observations while in the field, or in the natural habitat of the animal and away from a lab. They use this observation data to make generalizations about animal behavior. This activity will allow students to practice conducting observations at timed intervals and then draw conclusions from the data they collect.

Objectives:

- Students will conduct timed observations of animals.
- Students will record behavior of animals at regular intervals.
- Students will summarize their observations into percentages and pie chart format.

Principles and Standards for School Mathematics*
(National Council of Teachers of Mathematics, 2000)

- Standard 4: Measurement
- Standard 5: Data Analysis and Probability
- Standard 9: Communication
- Standard 10: Connections

Procedures

1. Before the visit, provide students with short video clips or publications that show scientists observing animals in the wild. Explain that for scientists to understand animal behavior, they have to spend some time watching the animals and taking notes.

2. If possible, allow students the opportunity to select the animal they would like to observe. This will be based on the animals present at the site, information that can be obtained from the Internet or by a preparation visit before the field trip. Assign animals prior to the trip and provide students with a sample of the data collection sheet ahead of time to allow them to familiarize themselves with the format.

3. In preparation for the visit, practice taking notes at timed intervals. One preparation activity would be to sit outside and watch students on a particular piece of play equipment. Every two minutes, ask students to describe how many students are using the equipment as well as how they are using it. Results should be discussed as a class, as should types of abbreviations that can facilitate quick note taking.

4. At the site, have students arrange themselves around the animal habitat. Each group should be provided with a clipboard with several data sheets and a pencil. The adult in charge should have a timer or watch that can measure one- or two-minute intervals. Younger students may need more time between recorded observations than older students due to the speed at which they can write.

5. Before the timing, have students record general observations such as the time of day, weather, number of animals, and general habitat structure. Before the timing begins, they should select one animal within the exhibition that they will focus on.

6. The adult/teacher should tell students to begin their fifteen-minute observation by recording exactly what their animal is doing (e.g., eating, sleeping, resting, playing, etc.). After each minute passes, the adult will call "time" and students will record another behavior. Some students may see these behaviors change, others may see their animal resting the whole time. That's okay! That's very much like the work of a real scientist.

7. After the fifteen minutes, provide time for students to explore the other areas of the learning site.

8. Back in the classroom, assist students with adding up the total number of times they saw each behavior and drawing conclusions as to which behavior was most common. They can create a final report on their findings by creating a poster, multimedia project, or oral presentation that will serve as the final evaluation piece.

*Standards are listed with the permission of the National Council of Teachers of Mathematics (NCTM). NCTM does not endorse the content or validity of these alignments.

Evaluation Rubric

Final Project	1	2	3
Data Presentation	Data presented inaccurately; calculations contain errors.	Some data are presented accurately, but there are some calculation errors.	Data are presented accurately; there are no calculation errors.
Conclusions	Students' conclusions are not supported by the data.	Some student conclusions are supported by the data, others are not based in observations.	Student conclusions are well grounded in observational data, with no unsupported conclusions.
Neatness/ Preparedness	Students' project shows little effort in the areas of neatness or advance preparation.	Students' project demonstrates some advanced planning and effort in the area of neatness and presentation.	Students' final project is neat, well planned, and demonstrates a high degree of preparedness.

Extension

Data can be entered into an electronic spreadsheet and several types of graphs can be generated. Students can discuss which type of graph best summarizes the information. This can lead into a more detailed discussion of what types of graphs are best for what kinds of data.

Helpful Web Sites

Citizen Science Projects

This site outlines wildlife research projects that are seeking the public's help in collecting data.

http://www.citzensci.com

Cornell Laboratory of Ornithology

This site provides information on birds of the United States as well as projects on local birds that students can assist with.

http://www.birds.cornell.edu

Earthwatch

This nonprofit organization provides information on different research projects on wildlife across the globe.

http://www.earthwatch.org

Cemeteries

In the last chapter, we explored methods of using cemetery studies to support the elementary social studies curriculum. Through basic operations students can gather important census information for the local community.

One element that is standard on nearly all gravestones is the presence of dates. By exploring these dates, students can draw conclusions about the age of the town, as well as demographic data of its inhabitants. Chapter 4 reviews special considerations for field trips to cemeteries in order to ensure a positive experience for all involved. It will be helpful to review that information before moving forward with the following activities.

K–2ND GRADE ACTIVITY: HOW OLD?

This activity will build student familiarity with using numerical data to solve problems and answer questions. Through an open-ended scavenger hunt, students will practice number sense as well as basic operations in addition and subtraction as age appropriate.

Objectives

- Students will locate dates and ages on gravestones as part of an open-ended scavenger hunt.
- Students will perform basic addition and subtraction using data from gravestones.

Principles and Standards for School Mathematics*
(National Council of Teachers of Mathematics, 2000).

- Standard 1: Number and Operations
- Standard 9: Communication
- Standard 10: Connections

Procedures

1. Before the visit, lead a discussion with students on the different ways numbers can tell us about our community. Examples might include the total number of people living in the town (population), the average age of people within a town, or even the oldest living resident. Brainstorm with students about dates that are important to them. What is an example of a very old date? What year were they born?

2. In preparation for the visit, create an open-ended scavenger hunt that will encourage students to explore the different numbers they might encounter during a cemetery visit, from gravestone dates to the location's address. Sample scavenger hunt tasks include the following:
   a. Find a gravestone from before you were born. Locate an example of the date 1913.
   b. What is the address of the cemetery?
   c. Can you find an example of someone who lived to be eighty years old or older?
      When creating questions, it is important to take into consideration the developmental level of the children. Though it is possible students will encounter a children's section during their visit, questions that focus on children that have passed can create unnecessary discomfort and are not recommended. Teachers will need to rely on their best judgment in creating a scavenger hunt well designed for the needs of their students

3. At the cemetery, place students in cooperative groups with an adult chaperone. For kindergarten and first-grade students, working as a group to do a single

*Standards are listed with the permission of the National Council of Teachers of Mathematics (NCTM). NCTM does not endorse the content or validity of these alignments.

scavenger hunt might be the best option. Second graders may welcome the opportunity to complete their own activity sheet with a minimum of adult support beyond simple safety supervision. Subtraction of four-digit numbers to identify ages may require some scaffolding from adult chaperones, or use of a calculator depending on the grade level of the students.

4. Provide adult chaperones with disposable or digital cameras to take photographs of students working, as well as the gravestones that meet the different criteria of the scavenger hunt. These can be used to create a bulletin board, send a thank-you note to the cemetery's administration, or for assessment purposes demonstrating an understanding of number sense.

5. Before leaving the cemetery, gather the class together for a brief discussion of their discoveries. This is also a chance to answer any questions students may have, or clear up any misconceptions about the experience before going home to share with parents.

6. Back in the classroom, collect student activity sheets and lead a final follow-up discussion about any patterns they noticed, questions that were difficult to answer, or dates that were difficult to find. Encourage them to look for dates and numbers each time they are out with their family, from a building cornerstone commemorating the construction of an important structure to the date a business was started.

Evaluation Rubric

Evaluation Rubric	No Credit	Credit
Scavenger Hunt	Student was off task and did not contribute to or complete the scavenger hunt activity sheet.	Student participated in completing the scavenger hunt activity sheet.

Modification

Younger children will be most successful with a high degree of scaffolding during the visit. Providing parent chaperones with a portable whiteboard or chalkboard will facilitate making needed calculations and provide students with needed visuals.

3RD–5TH GRADE ACTIVITY: SUPER SLEUTHING

Older students will be able to use data from gravestones to answer questions of personal interest as well as draw conclusions regarding town demographics based on data they have collected themselves (see the vignette at the end of this chapter).

Objectives

- Students will conduct an original research project utilizing data from cemetery gravestones.
- Students will create a presentation board outlining their research question, data collected, and final results.
- Students will present their discoveries to the class through oral presentation.

Principles and Standards for School Mathematics*
(National Council of Teachers of Mathematics, 2000)

- Standard 1: Number and Operations
- Standard 5: Data Analysis and Probability
- Standard 6: Problem Solving
- Standard 10: Connections

Procedures

1. Before the visit, lead a class discussion on demographic information and what numbers can tell us about a community. Practice simple calculations such as percentage of males and females within the class, average age of students, or month containing the most student birthdays.

2. In preparation for the visit, place students in groups of four. Inform groups that they will be able to pick a research question of their choice working directly with numerical data. Most students will find sample questions helpful. With younger students, focusing on a more historic area of a local cemetery may be easier and raise fewer feelings of discomfort than a location with recent graves. The location of your data collection will guide the sample questions you provide, but some examples include the following:
   a. What was the average age people reached in the 1800s?
   b. Did one month seem to have more deaths than another month?
   c. Breaking the 1800s into decades, what decade had the most deaths?
   d. Do students encounter more deceased males or females?
   e. What was the most common first name in the year _____?

3. To prepare for data collection during the field trip, work with individual groups to assist with data collection design. For example, comparing males and females would require an activity sheet with two columns and room for tally marks. For studies focused on months of the year, activity sheets with twelve spaces for tally marks, each labeled with a month, is the best design. Once this has been decided, help students actually create the data sheet and prepare for the visit.

4. During the visit, each group will need an adult chaperone to guide the data collection. This facilitation is critical both for accuracy in data collection and to ensure students exhibit respectful behavior within the cemetery. Have an adult available to address immediately any concerns or questions that come up during the visit that may cause feelings of discomfort on the part of students.

5. Before leaving the cemetery, meet as a class briefly to ensure each group has collected the data they need for their final project. At this time, any special concerns or questions can be addressed so students go home feeling good about their experience.

6. Back in the classroom, provide time for groups to work with the data they collected. Provide calculators as appropriate for computation and tools to create graphs, either on paper or with the help of a computer graphing program. Provide each group with a presentation board in order to communicate their question and discoveries, remembering to display all calculations in addition to their final results. Once all presentation boards are completed, students will orally present their projects to the rest of the class, with each student participating. These finished projects and corresponding oral presentations will serve as the final assessment piece.

---

*Standards are listed with the permission of the National Council of Teachers of Mathematics (NCTM). NCTM does not endorse the content or validity of these alignments.

Evaluation Rubric

	1	2	3
Data Presentation	Student was off task and disrespectful of cemetery grounds.	Student was partially engaged, but may have been off task or behaved disrespectfully at times.	Student was engaged and conducted explorations respectfully.
Poster	Poster has very little required information and/or there are significant errors.	Poster highlights some aspects of the project accurately, but there are also errors and/or omissions.	Poster accurately summarizes all aspects of the project: question, calculations, and results.
Oral Presentation	Student is not prepared and does not demonstrate appropriate effort.	Student is partially prepared, but may need assistance from peers; student demonstrates good effort in presentation style.	Student demonstrates comfort with the material and is well prepared; student demonstrates great effort, using good voice quality and making eye contact.

Modification

Rather than individual projects, the class can focus on a single research question, each gathering a portion of the data. Back in the classroom, the teacher can scaffold the data analysis, completing this portion as a whole-class discussion.

Helpful Web Sites

Cemetery Transcription Network

This site provides general information about cemeteries and grave markers, as well as a search engine to explore specific details about cemeteries around the world.

http://www.interment.net

United States Census Bureau

This site provides demographic statistics for the nation and has a special site for educators with lesson plans on how to incorporate census data into the K–12 classroom.

http://www.census.gov

Note: Many online resources for cemetery studies are state specific. A simple search will easily provide several Web sites specific to your geographic region.

ALSO CONSIDER . . .

Other field trip options to support math learning include

Farmers' Market: These locations provide experiences with measurement and currency, as well as interaction with small business owners. With special planning, students may be able to communicate with an exhibitor regarding the role mathematics plays in all aspects of the business, from accounting and bills payable to making change at the venue.

Pharmacy: The pharmacy is one location where getting numbers and measurements correct is a matter of good health. Arranging for a visit to a local pharmacy and a conversation with a pharmacist or pharmacy technician can support students in learning mathematical concepts within an authentic context.

Subway/Train Station: In these locations, the concept of time is critical. Providing students with a train schedule and asking them to track arriving and departing trains for a set period of time provides an opportunity for calculating elapsed time. In addition, older students can explore issues of statistics as they calculate the percentage of on-time arrivals and departures.

Pizza Parlor: From area of a circle to addition of fractions, a simple pizza provides numerous opportunities for advanced calculations. Encourage students to use math to determine how much sauce is used per pizza or the number of pounds of cheese that need to be ordered. Challenge them to determine the greatest number of slices they can create from one pizza.

Vignette: Date Detectives

Ms. Gilliland asked students to find a place in the shade to sit so they could go over the activity plan for the day. Students found the members of their team and sat together with their clipboards on their laps. Someone suggested they leave all their backpacks by one large tree. "No one would steal anything from a cemetery, would they?" Kimberly whispered to her partner.

Ms. Gilliland reviewed her behavioral expectations. "Okay, you'll remember we talked about the importance of respect within a cemetery, right?" The students nodded enthusiastically, ready to get to work and have the orientation done with. "Okay, then, you know your task. You'll have fifteen minutes to work before our first check point. Do you all know what location you are working in?" The students nodded as they quickly stood up and made their way across the cemetery grounds.

As the students splintered off, the groundskeeper came over to greet Ms. Gilliland. "They're really excited about this project, aren't they?" he chuckled.

Ms. Gilliland smiled. "Thank you again for your understanding. They know this is a place for their research and promise to be respectful."

(Continued)

Ms. Gilliland did a quick visual check to ensure that each student group was sticking close to their adult chaperone as well as steering clear of anyone visiting the grave of a loved one. Once she was convinced all students were on track, she wandered over to the first group to see how the data collection was going.

"Is that an 8 or a 9?"

"I don't know, it's really hard to read, But I think it's a 9."

Katie did some quick calculations in her head. "Wow, another person who died before he turned 30!" Katie shook her head. "That's younger than my dad!"

"And look, it was the 1800s again. Wow, it sure was hard to stay alive back then!" Gary comments.

Jun made another tally mark in the "30s" column on his data collection sheet. Gary made a tally mark in the column reserved for the nineteenth century on his data sheet. Heidi continued writing a complete data record including name, date of birth, and date of death for each grave they visited. They would be responsible for creating a graph of all their data back in the classroom as well as a map of their section of the cemetery.

The team continued the process at several more gravestones. Suddenly Katie got a big smile on her face and turned toward Ms. Gilliland. "I'm starting to get really good at quickly figuring out the ages in my head. It's so much easier to find the difference between two numbers when it actually means something . . . like how old someone was."

Ms. Gilliland smiled back at her and headed off to the newer section of the cemetery. With gravestones that are easier to read, the group was almost done and would soon be ready to gather some data from inside the mausoleum.

Data Sheet 4 Class Calculations

How Many Animals?

Investigator:_____   Date:_____

Types of Animal	Tallies	Totals
mammals		
birds		
reptiles		
amphibians		
fish		

Data Summary: Bar Graph

Number of Animals

Mam   **Birds**   **Rep**   **Amph**   **Fish**

Animal Types

6

An Artistic Eye

Fine Art Explorations

The study of fine arts is an important component of the classroom curriculum. From interpretive dance to techniques of painting, the fine arts are not only a field where students can learn to express themselves, but also to appreciate the creative expression of others. It is also a lens through which to explore a world larger than the immediate community. Howard Gardner (1991) reminds us that artistic expression is one of many different pathways through which children make meaning. Though the relevance of fine arts to the classroom curriculum is clear, many schools do not house the resources or expertise to create a rich fine arts curriculum. This is where field trip destinations can fill a significant void.

FROM COLORING BOOKS TO COMPOSITION

As we encourage students to explore their creative side, it is imperative to draw connections between student projects and established art theory. Just as students should be conducting historical research as a social scientist and solving authentic problems as a mathematician, it is critical that they are allowed to explore their creativity as a true artist would.

One of the potential pitfalls of arts education at the elementary level is the potential for art activities to take on a strictly craft focus. While there is always a place for Styrofoam, glitter, and tongue depressor crafts in the elementary classroom, it is important also to provide a more academic grounding in art theory and technique, to provide a real-world context for students.

For example, magazine collages are a favorite of young children and a staple of many elementary classroom projects. However, they need not stand alone as a simple cut-and-paste activity. By sharing the work of artists who work in mixed media, such as Robert Rauschenberg, as well as some simple themes in composition before students get cutting, you can provide a context for your students' creations in line with the work of professional artists and established theory.

In order to create personally relevant experiences in the arts for students, it is necessary to include contemporary expressions. The elementary curriculum can sometimes get weighted with grand master painters, baroque compositions, and Balanchine ballet. Deconstructing jazz, viewing a performance of stomping, or exploring the work of local muralists can help make the arts more relevant to students whose exposure to traditional masters may be limited. This can also reinforce the importance of creativity and individuality to the core of artistic expression (Ross, 2005). After all, art explorations serve to prepare students not only to express themselves creatively through their own works of art, but also to analyze critically and evaluate creative expressions of others (Consortium of National Arts Education, 1994), be it the opening of a new exhibition or a performance from a new choreographer. Further, the fine arts are an important vehicle for expression using modalities different from the written and verbal emphasis of the traditional classroom, and specifically an opportunity to "develop the full child" (Koff, 2000, p. 31).

A WORD ON PROFESSIONAL PERFORMANCES

There are few things that can take the place of seeing the ballet, opera, or Shakespeare performed by a professional company or community group. Any opportunity to take advantage of this exposure should be taken. Some companies and theaters will have discounts for students or even grants to allow for free viewings. Others may invite the community to dress rehearsals free of charge. For some educators, however, these types of field trips may be out of reach. For this reason, the remainder of the chapter will focus on exposure to the arts that is accessible to the average elementary educator.

MAKING CONNECTIONS: INFORMAL LEARNING AND THE FINE ARTS

Art Museums

Even the smallest art museum will provide students with exposure to a range of different artists and a variety of artistic media. From sculpture and mosaic to oil and acrylic, a visit to an art museum is a wonderful way to conduct a survey with your students and help them discover the types of work they are most interested in.

K–2ND GRADE ACTIVITY: WHAT DO *YOU* THINK?

The first step toward art appreciation is providing students with the opportunity to interpret what they see and share their thoughts about the work. This activity supports oral language development as it encourages students to interpret works of art in relation to their own experiences.

Objectives

- Students will view different pieces of art.
- Students will orally explain to a peer what they think the artist was thinking or feeling while creating a particular piece of art.
- Students will share with a peer their own thoughts of the piece.

National Standards for Arts Education*
(Consortium of National Arts Education, 1994)

- Content Standard #5: Reflecting upon and assessing the characteristics and merits of their work and the work of others

Procedures

1. Before visiting the art museum, remind students that artists create works of art for many different reasons. Explain that the work of artists will often contain details that refer to historic events or personal aspects of the artist's life. Finish the discussion by explaining that people may differ in the types of art they enjoy. These differences are natural and you are excited to learn more about the types of artwork they find especially enjoyable. It can be helpful to model this discussion using a large reproduction of a particular artwork within the classroom setting.

2. While at the museum, place students in groups of two. Though you may navigate the museum with several pairs in one large group, the oral discussion of the activity will take place within these assigned pairs.

3. As you navigate the museum, pause within each gallery to allow students to view and discuss a piece of their choosing. They should express to their partner possible answers to several questions:
   a. What was the artist thinking when he or she created the piece?
   b. What might have been happening around the artist when the piece was created?
   c. Is this a piece you would like to hang in your home? Why or why not?

4. During these paired discussions, the teacher and adult chaperones can circulate among students and help guide their oral discussion, assisting them with noticing small details within the artwork to support their stance. Adults can also help by recording student comments together with information on the artist or work. If the museum allows no-flash photography, pictures of students engaged in discussion can be taken by the teacher or accompanying adults.

5. Back in the classroom, the teacher can create a bulletin board with student comments combined with images of the works pulled from the Internet or perhaps using inexpensive postcards sold within the museum gift store.

*Source: From *National Standards for Arts Education*, developed by the Consortium of National Arts Education Associations. Copyright © 1994 by Music Educators National Conference. Used with permission.

Evaluation Rubric

	No Credit	Credit
Field Trip Discussion	Student does not attempt discussion of the artwork with peers.	Student makes an attempt to discuss with peers their thoughts on the artwork.

Modification

If at all possible, pair English learners with a peer who speaks the same primary language to encourage active discussion. For students who may be shy about communicating their thoughts with peers, teacher mediation of the discussion may be necessary.

3RD–5TH GRADE ACTIVITY: ARTISTICALLY INSPIRED

Many artists are inspired by the work of others, for instance in the use of a particular medium or a thematic subject area. In this activity, students record details of some of their favorite works and then use similar materials and themes for their own artistic expression back in the classroom.

Objectives

- Students will observe a particular artwork and record the techniques and materials used in its creation.
- Students will record information on the thematic focus of the piece.
- Students will create an original piece of artwork inspired by the piece observed at the museum.

National Standards for Arts Education
(Consortium of National Arts Education, 1994)

- Content Standard #1: Understanding and applying media, techniques, and processes

Procedures

1. Before the visit, share with students that many famous artists find inspiration and direction by observing the work of other artists. Spend some time discussing the difference between "being inspired" and "copying." For example, an artist who is inspired may use the same mixture of newspaper and acrylic paint as his or her mentor, but do so in an individual style.

2. Explain that during their visit, they will identify a piece they really enjoy and make notes on how the piece was created. These notes will be used to create a piece of original art after they return from the field trip.

3. During the visit, provide students with notebooks and pencils in order to take notes. Circulate among students to assist them in their note taking and point out how some museum labels can provide information on the media utilized by the artist. Be sure they include the artist and the name of the piece for later evaluation purposes. A sample data sheet is provided at the end of this chapter (Data Sheet 5).

4. Encourage students to record information on several pieces. An artist will often begin moving in one direction with their work and then find they would like to create something totally different. By recording lots of information, students will have a great deal of choice on their final creation.

5. Photographs are often allowed within art museums as long as a flash is not used. Check with the museum in advance on the official policy. If photographs are not allowed, many museums have gift shops that sell inexpensive postcards of key pieces. If photographs are allowed, take pictures of the pieces students have selected as their inspiration. These images can help guide students during their creation phase.

6. Back in the classroom, provide students with all the materials they will need to create an original piece of artwork. The final artwork will serve as the assessment piece. Suggested supplies include the following:

Canvas boards

Paint (student-grade acrylic paint)

Colored chalk/pastels

Colored pencils

Charcoal

Watercolors

Art paper

Magazines for collages

Clay

Miscellaneous "found" objects (string, sticks, pieces of wood, etc.)

Evaluation Rubric

	1	2	3
Completed Artwork	Student project has no tie to the artwork observed within the museum environment.	Student work is somewhat related to an observed museum piece, but either does not display enough originality or does not parallel the artistic methods of the target piece.	Student work utilizes similar media, techniques, and/or themes as the museum piece while maintaining originality.

Extension

Because of the student-choice aspect of this activity, there is room for all students to demonstrate success and limited modifications will be necessary. An exciting extension would be to create a mini-museum and encourage other students to come view your class's creations.

Helpful Web Sites

The J. Paul Getty Trust

This site will allow students to search art collections as well as learn about the scholarly research conducted within art museums.

http://www.getty.edu

The Metropolitan Museum of Art: Works of Art
Students can engage in online activities and investigations, as well as view images of temporary and permanent collections.
http://www.metmuseum.org/Works_of_Art

Smithsonian American Art Museum
This multifaceted site includes online exhibitions, tips on researching art, and an "ask an expert" feature.
http://americanart.si.edu

Public Murals

Examples of wall murals can be found in almost any community. Within our urban communities, there may be a mural on every block. Some schools even have murals right on campus. Viewing and exploring the motivation behind public murals nicely integrates themes in art theory and social commentary. Whether professionally commissioned or completed by children, murals can teach students to learn to "read" the story of an image.

K–2ND GRADE ACTIVITY: WHAT DOES IT *SAY?*

Objectives

- Students will discuss with a peer the message behind a public mural.
- Students will design a mural for their school that delivers a message they feel is important.

National Standards for Arts Education
(Consortium of National Arts Education, 1994)

- Content Standard #4: Understanding the visual arts in relation to history and cultures

Procedures

1. Before the visit, share images of murals with students and lead a discussion of what messages the murals were meant to share. Internet resources can assist with this step.

2. Arrange to visit one or more murals with the class. The best choice is a location with several murals all within walking distance, if this is a possibility. While in front of the mural, encourage students to discuss what message they feel the mural is sharing with the community. Be sure to validate a variety of responses and interject with information you might have about the history of the community that predates your young students.

3. Back in the classroom, revisit the discussion. Ask students to suggest messages they feel would be important to display on the school grounds, to tell visitors something important about the school. Provide each child with a large (11″ × 17″) piece of white paper and markers or crayons to design their own mural based on the discussion.

4. End the activity by allowing students to explain their design to their peers. Find a spot within the classroom to display completed student work. Final assessment

will be based on discussion during the field trip as well as the original mural design.

Evaluation Rubric

	No Credit	Credit
Field Trip Discussion	Student does not participate in class discussion and does not demonstrate on-task listening behavior.	Student is an active member of the discussion, either by sharing their own opinion or simply by being a good listener, actively focused on the teacher and peers who are speaking.
Original Mural Design	Student does not create an original mural.	Student creates an original mural design and can explain the concept either to the teacher privately, to a friend, or in front of the class.

Modification

For students who may not be comfortable sharing their work with the entire class, encourage sharing within a small group or with one classmate.

3RD–5TH GRADE ACTIVITY: CAPTURING THE COMMUNITY

Community murals often address issues of significant concern to residents. They may memorialize tragic situations and struggles or celebrate significant achievements. Older students will be more aware of community issues as well as concerns at a more global level. This activity builds on the activity for grade levels K–2 but asks students to cooperatively design a mural that addresses a major issue within the community.

Objectives

- Students will visit a mural that captures a critical message and discuss it as a class.
- Students will cooperatively design an original mural addressing an important concern within their community or at a global level.

National Standards for Arts Education (Consortium of National Arts Education, 1994)

- Content Standard #4: Understanding the visual arts in relation to history and cultures

Procedures

1. Before the visit, share images of murals with students and lead a discussion of what messages the murals were meant to share.

2. Arrange to visit one or more murals that express important community views or controversial messages, or memorialize historic actions or events.

3. During the visit, discuss in depth what messages the students take away from the murals. If they could add to or change the mural, what would they like to see done? Encourage them to take notes and bring a digital camera to take photos of the work.

4. Back in the classroom, revisit the discussion using student comments and images as a guide. Ask students to share verbally additional messages they feel are important to the community. Write these messages on the board as they are shared.

5. After the discussion, allow students to choose a message they would like to design a mural around. Place students in cooperative groups based on these choices and provide students with poster boards to create their mural. Be sure to provide scratch paper for initial sketches as well as markers and other art materials to create a visually dynamic display.

6. Have students orally share their designs and find a place to display student designs, either in the classroom or elsewhere on the school grounds. Finished designs will serve as the final assessment piece together with student participation during the field trip itself.

Evaluation Rubric

	No Credit	Credit
Field Trip Discussion	Student does not participate in class discussion and does not demonstrate on-task listening behavior.	Student is an active member of the discussion, either by sharing their own opinion or simply by being a good listener, actively focused on the teacher and peers who are speaking.
Cooperative Mural Design	Student does not create an original mural within a cooperative group.	Student creates an original mural design as part of a cooperative group.

Extension

Explore the possibility of actually using student designs for murals on the school site. Another option is to connect with a community mural organization and share student designs for potential use within the community.

Helpful Web Site

Groundswell

This site provides images of local museum projects within the New York City area.

http://www.groundswellmural.org

Note: Due to the community-based nature of mural projects, it will be most appropriate to search out Web sites linked to local organizations.

Local Dance Schools

Though not all cities host an internationally known dance company, many do have a dance school or two. Most dance schools have various levels of instruction, and being able to observe a high-level ballet class is a great way to expose students to dance technique without the high price of ballet tickets. In addition, dance schools often offer a variety of different types of dance instruction, providing students with the opportunity to compare flamenco with jazz with ballroom dancing. Many dance schools have community performances or recitals. Tickets for these events are usually quite affordable and there may be a chance your students can observe a dress rehearsal with no ticket charge.

K–2ND GRADE ACTIVITY: WHO CAN I DANCE LIKE?

Watching a live performance or dance class is a little different from most of the activities in this book. Many of the ideas, activity sheets, and experience guides discussed thus far might create a distraction in the hands of young learners who are being encouraged to watch the performance with good manners and respect. For that reason, the activity described here relies heavily on recall of the performance and its overall impression on students.

Objectives

- Students will observe a live dance performance.
- Students will kinesthetically re-create the dance experience they witnessed, with emphasis on an individual dancer they most want to emulate.

National Standards for Arts Education
(Consortium of National Arts Education, 1994)

- Content Standard #1: Identifying and demonstrating movement elements and skills in performing dance

Procedures

1. Before the performance or class observation, prepare students for what they will see. Most dance schools will have information on their Web sites or in hard copy about the type of dancing that is their focus.

2. Review polite behavior so students will know what is expected of them during the performance. If the class is especially energetic, a trial run might be in order.

3. Ask students to pay special attention during the performance, as they will be asked to replicate one of their favorite parts back in the classroom. After watching the whole group for a while, they may want to select one person to pay special attention to.

4. Directly after the performance, assist in reinforcing what students observed by reviewing key parts of the performance. Ask students to add information about what they enjoyed or thought was memorable.

5. Back in the classroom, provide students with the opportunity to replicate some of the movements they observed. To alleviate shyness for some students, begin as a whole group. Ask one student to demonstrate while the rest follow along. If there are students who are especially focused on performing, they can be provided with some "solo time" after the group demonstrations. The final assessment piece will be student participation in the dance demonstration.

Evaluation Rubric

	1	2	3
Dance Demonstration	Student is off task and/or dances in an inappropriate or silly manner.	Student attempts appropriate dance performance yet at times acts inappropriately, with giggles or inappropriate movements.	Student makes a proper attempt to perform dance in line with the performance observed.

Modification

To accommodate students with physical disabilities, remind the class that dance can involve head and hand movements, and can incorporate the use of mobility equipment such as a wheelchair or a cane. The Axis Dance Company, comprised of dancers with and without disabilities, is one resource to assist with this (http://www.axisdance.org).

3RD–5TH GRADE ACTIVITY: UNDERSTANDING MOVEMENT

At this age, students are beginning to understand more about how their bodies move. As they watch dancers perform, it is natural and important for them to notice the special talent, strength, and flexibility dancers demonstrate. This activity will ask students to make sketches of key movements or positions and then replicate the isolated movements back in the classroom.

Objectives

- Students observe dancers and make two or three stick figure sketches of dance positions.
- Students will ask a partner to replicate the movements with the sketch as a guide.

National Standards for Arts Education
(Consortium of National Arts Education, 1994)

- Content Standard #1: Identifying and demonstrating movement elements and skills in performing dance

Procedures

1. Before the performance or class observation, prepare students for what they will see. Most dance schools will have information on their Web sites or in hard copy about the type of dancing that is their focus.

2. Lead a discussion about how dancers tell stories using body movements. If possible, share video clips from different types of dance checked out from a local video store. Inform students that as they are watching the dance demonstration, they will be making very simple stick figure sketches of two or three dance positions they find especially interesting.

3. Directly after the performance, check to make sure all students have recorded at least two illustrations. For students who did not accomplish this step, assist them in both recall of the performance and creation of a simple stick figure.

4. Back in the classroom, find a place where the entire class will have room to move about. This might be inside a school gym or on the schoolyard. Place students in pairs and ask them to take turns interpreting each other's stick figure sketches. This should be an energetic activity and expect that the volume may rise.

5. After working in pairs, bring the class together and ask if any students would like to demonstrate some of the movements from their sketches. The final assessment piece will be the student's attempt to replicate the movement captured in their partner's sketches.

Evaluation Rubric

	No Credit	Credit
Replication of Dance Sketch	Student does not participate in making sketches and/or in replicating a partner's sketch.	Student makes an attempt both to make sketches and to replicate a partner's sketch.

Modification

The same modifications for students with disabilities at Grades K–2 would be applicable at this level. If they are physically unable to replicate the complete movement, demonstrating with just arm movement or a tilt of the head would be appropriate.

Helpful Web Sites

Alvin Ailey American Dance Theater: Video Clips
This site allows students to view video of choreography performed by members of this highly respected modern dance company.
http://www.alvinailey.org/page.php?p=mediad&t=video&sec=multimedia

American Ballet Theater: Dictionary of Ballet Terms
This site includes video of different ballet movements along with written definitions.
http://www.abt.org/education/dictionary

The Kennedy Center: Artsedge
This site includes an excellent searchable database of lessons connected to the performing arts.
http://artsedge.kennedy-center.org

Music Supply Stores

Unfortunately, many school music programs have been cut due to limited funding. With that change, students are often less familiar with orchestral music. There is no need to visit the symphony, however, to learn about different types of musical instruments. A local music supply store may be persuaded to provide students with a brief introduction to their stock and the opportunity to touch, see, and hear a variety of musical instruments and printed music. You may find that a store that caters to your local neighborhood or one that offers lessons to children may be more apt to allow a visit.

K-2ND GRADE ACTIVITY: ALL ABOUT INSTRUMENTS

Learning about different instruments and the sounds they make is a first step toward understanding more complex ideas of musical composition and theory (see the vignette at the end of this chapter).

Objectives

- Students will compare and contrast different musical instruments.
- Students will hear the different sounds musical instruments make.

National Standards for Arts Education
(Consortium of National Arts Education, 1994)

- Content Standard #6: Listening to, analyzing, and describing music

Procedures

1. Make arrangements with a local music store for a visit. You may find that offering to come in before the store normally opens is the best way to avoid interfering with regular customers.

2. Before going on the trip, provide some exposure to different musical instruments, using images from the Internet and playing musical snippets for students.

3. At the music store, begin by reviewing the rules of touching. It is probably best if students do not touch instruments without the assistance of an adult, but work with the store owner on what he or she feels is best.

4. Encourage students to walk around the store with a partner and identify as many different instruments as they can. You can provide them with a musical instrument "field guide" or a collection of pictures that they check off as they encounter each type.

5. Gather students in one part of the store and initiate conversation on differences and similarities between the instruments they observed. It is best if instruments can be held up during the discussion, pointing to specific features as students share.

6. If possible, try to arrange for a store employee or musically talented friend to play a few notes from each instrument. The final assessment will be based on student participation during the field trip.

Evaluation Rubric

	1	2	3	4
Instrument Investigation	Student accomplishes none or 1 of the following elements: • actively explores the different instruments; • listens attentively during presentation; • explains how two instruments are similar; • explains how two instruments are different.	Student accomplishes 2 of the 4 elements.	Student accomplishes 3 of the 4 elements.	Student accomplishes all 4 elements.

Modifications

If you have students who are deaf or hearing impaired, you might want to ask permission for those children to touch each instrument as it is played in order to feel the different vibrations each creates. If you cannot find a music store to work with you, you may want to tap into the local junior high or high school music program as an alternative.

3RD–5TH GRADE ACTIVITY: SEEING MUSIC

Once students understand that different instruments make different sounds, giving them exposure to reading music is a sensible next step. This goes beyond simply naming notes to understanding that sheet music may look different for different instruments, that there may be different versions of the same song, or that some arrangements may be simpler than others to accommodate beginners.

Objectives

- Students will compare and contrast different types of printed music.
- Students will hear instruments played while following along with printed music.

National Standards for Arts Education
(Consortium of National Arts Education, 1994)

- Content Standard #5: Reading and noting music

Procedures

1. Before the field trip, provide students with examples of sheet music. Provide them with an example intended for use by a beginner and an example intended for use by a more accomplished musician. Discuss the similarities and differences.

2. During the visit, ask permission for students to freely explore the printed music. Remind students to treat the selection of music as they would a library. Discuss the importance of looking through books or sheet music carefully and putting them back in their original place on the display rack.

3. Provide students with a simple activity sheet or a blank journal to write down some of the things they notice as they compare different arrangements. Encourage them to work in cooperative groups. Move among the groups, providing assistance when needed.

4. If it can be arranged, have a music store staff member play students a couple of selections from different instruments and have students follow along with the printed music. It may be necessary to make needed copies of music available for students to follow along. It will be important to plan ahead for this need.

5. Back in the classroom, have students share their observations during a class discussion. This discussion together with the on-site exploration will serve as the final assessment piece.

Evaluation Rubric

	No Credit	Credit
On-site Exploration	Student does not participate in exploration of music during the field trip.	Student actively explores printed music within the cooperative group and takes notes; student listens attentively during presentation.
Class Discussion	Student does not participate.	Student participates in class discussion both by sharing and by listening attentively to peers.

Modification

For students with low vision, it is a simple step to enlarge portions of the printed music using a traditional copy machine. This may require advance planning with the store owner for previsit access and perhaps the opportunity to borrow the music in order to make needed copies.

Helpful Web Sites

Naxos: The Learning Zone

This classical music label has a site dedicated to supporting enjoyment of classical music, from composer biographies to tips on enjoying live music performances.

http://www.naxos.com/newdesign/flearning.files/blearning.htm

National Geographic Society: World Music

This site provides information on music from around the world as well as video and audio clips so students can see and hear the music performed. http://worldmusic.nationalgeographic.com/worldmusic/view/page.basic/home

University of Michigan: Instrument Encyclopedia

This site allows students to browse information about musical instruments by the type of instrument as well as the geographic region from which the instrument originated. http://www.si.umich.edu/chico/instrument

ALSO CONSIDER . . .

Other field trip options to support fine arts learning include

Private Art Galleries: Many communities may have private, for-profit art galleries that can serve as a field trip destination if a traditional art museum is not an option. These locations do not have admission fees so are a cost-effective option. Even if the art displayed is from an emerging artist, it can still provide an opportunity to practice interpretation and recognize the use of a variety of media. As these spaces are usually small and aimed at selling artwork, be sure to contact them in advance in order to determine the feasibility of a student visit.

Art Supply Store: With advance notice, art supply stores may gladly welcome budding artists into their stores for a guided tour. This can be a chance for students to learn the difference between acrylic and oil paint, how a canvas is stretched, or the process of papermaking. Providing a mock "budget" to buy supplies can link well to math standards.

Music Store: Some music stores provide the opportunity to listen to different albums before purchase. This creates a great opportunity for students to explore different types of music free of charge. It will be important to first call ahead to ensure that the store can accommodate a full class. It will also be necessary to put guidelines in place to guard against accessing albums containing lyrics that may upset parents of young children. Independent music stores may be better able, and more willing, to connect with local schools than larger chains, who may have to answer to corporate policy.

Dance Supply Store: For students without a dance background, the construction of a tap shoe or pointe shoe is a great mystery. Understanding the tools of a dancer is one way to better understand dance itself. A local dance supply store can provide insight into the "behind the scenes" aspect of the performing arts, from stage makeup to knee braces. These stores cater to the needs of both male and female dancers in all genres. A visit can help reinforce the range of people who dance for enjoyment or as a profession, as well as remind students of the diversity of dance genres.

Local High School: Whether it is an English teacher who is willing to share Shakespeare with students or a drama department willing to demonstrate staging or costume design, the local high school is an excellent resource. As members of the same district, the sense of community can assist in making that first step toward a partnership.

Vignette: Musical Investigations

"Hey look... here's a violin!" shouts first grader Hector.

"I found a violin, too!" Carrie comments.

"Me too! Me too!" chimes in Sarah. She then frowns. "But mine is so big!"

The teacher waits until the staff members can help students carefully gather up the three instruments and bring them to an open space in the front of the store. The staff members stand next to the teacher with the different instruments and the students sit cross-legged on the rug at their feet.

The teacher initiates discussion: "You had said you all found violins, but do these all look the same?"

"Noooooo," say the students in unison. And one boy quickly shoots up his hand.

"I think that one is a jello..."

"I think you mean cello, and you're right, Steven. Though they look similar, these three instruments have some differences, too, and they definitely have different names. I'm going to have Ms. Kelly record what we have to say about all these different instruments so we can discuss our discoveries when we are back in class. Ms. Kelly, did you get down Steven's comment?"

Ms. Kelly, the teaching assistant for the class, nods and holds up the clipboard to show the class she is recording their discussion.

"What are some other things you notice about the size and shape of these instruments?"

The children take turns commenting on physical attributes of the instruments, as Ms. Kelly writes down their observations. The students have so much to say, she has to slow them down a couple of times in order to record all of their discoveries.

After several minutes, the teacher switches gears. "Mr. Klondike, do you have a staff member who could play a couple of notes from each of the instruments?" Mr. Klondike smiles and offers to do the demonstration himself. Before he begins, the teacher asks students to close their eyes. He plays a few notes each with the violin, the cello, and the viola. The students close their eyes and listen to the different tones each instrument produces. When he is finished, the teacher asks students to take a minute and discuss with a partner what they noticed about the music they heard. When they are done sharing with their partner, the teacher asks for volunteers to share with the whole class. Ms. Kelly is kept very busy with a whole other set of comments to record.

It is the end of the visit and the students are reluctant to go. They line up slowly, hoping that stalling can buy more time in the music store. "Friends," the teacher prompts, "can you thank Mr. Klondike and his staff for coming in early for our visit? They usually don't open until 10:00, so this was a very special treat."

"Thank you, Mr. Klondike and friends!" the children recite dutifully before going back to whispering excitedly about the different instruments they got to hear.

"I'm going to ask my mom for a piano!" one child exclaims as they file out of the store and walk back to their school just a few blocks away.

"You're welcome," Mr. Klondike answers. He can't help thinking, it won't be long before his three-year-old will be going on field trips herself!

Data Sheet 5 Artistic Inspiration

Learning From a Master

Art Student:_____   Date:_____

Target Artist:_____

What materials does the artist use to create?

_____

_____

_____

Draw a sketch of one or more works below.

What makes this artist's work unique or different from the other pieces?

_____

_____

_____

What other information would be important to know?

_____

_____

_____

7

Access for All

*Successful Field Trip
Experiences for Everyone*

Field trip destinations are perhaps the most authentic learning context students can experience. Students with diverse learning needs, such as English learners and those who receive special education services, can perhaps benefit most significantly from these experiences. However, even the best intentioned teacher may be faced with a location that is not physically accessible for all students, a language barrier that results in an unsigned permission slip, or a student with a social/emotional disorder being fearful of joining in the yearly field trip. This chapter emphasizes the critical role that field trips can play in the education of students with disabilities as well as our English learners. In addition, some special considerations are highlighted to help support an inclusive and successful visit.

SPECIAL CONSIDERATIONS: ENGLISH LEARNERS

Field trip experiences are a wonderful way for English learners to develop vocabulary as well as gain experience with their surrounding community. Authentic context and real objects and specimens are critical tools for language development. Field trip locations are rich in both of these elements. In addition, many English learners may come from families who are new to the surrounding community and may not have had the opportunity to explore local resources and cultural institutions. In fact, for many English learners the school field trip to a local zoo, historic home, or museum may be their first or even only experience with these resources (see Student Story A).

Tip 1: Getting Permission

Sometimes English learners may not be granted parental permission to go on a school field trip simply because parents did not understand the permission slip. This is not simply a matter of translating the language on the slip but also educating parents on the role a field trip can play in their child's schooling. Parents who may be new to the United States may need additional information or details provided, particularly regarding issues of safety and supervision. It may be necessary to offer reassurance that the child will always be supervised and that there is no additional fee for the trip. A quick phone call explaining the permission slip and requesting a signature can be helpful if you have concerns about the literacy level of parents without creating an awkward situation. Enlisting the help of a room-parent or PTA representative can be helpful in explaining the upcoming trip. Inviting parents along as chaperones is also an excellent way to make that connection.

Tip 2: Ask About Special Materials

Many informal learning institutions have written materials, such as visitor guides or exhibit pamphlets, available in a variety of languages. Just one example is the Getty Center of Los Angeles, which provides visitor information in ten different languages. Sharing these resources with the entire class, and especially English learners, before a visit can help familiarize students with elements of the destination before arrival and better prepare them to be actively involved in planned activities. These materials can also be helpful in supporting parent chaperones so they too can be active contributors to the experience.

Tip 3: During the Visit Details

Many teachers are comfortable with the modifications necessary to help English learners succeed in the classroom. These same types of modifications will ensure successful exploration during a field trip. Creating tasks that allow students to communicate orally and with drawings is one way to meet the needs of English learners who may still be acquiring English writing skills. Grouping students with bilingual peers or parents can allow for in-depth discussion of exhibits and activities for students still developing English fluency. Creating an original study guide for the visit with images of exhibits downloaded from the Internet, together with a word bank of key terms in English, will help reinforce any new vocabulary.

Tip 4: Family Follow-Up

A number of studies have indicated that museums are often less visited by culturally and linguistically diverse families (Korn, 2005; Melber, 2003; Smithsonian Institution, 2001). Reasons are many and may include issues of high admission fees, English-only visitor materials, or a general lack of familiarity with local offerings and methods of navigating these unfamiliar spaces. However, research also indicates that repeat visitation to a field trip location can significantly increase cognitive gains on the part of students (Price & Hein, 1991). Sending home information to families about the visit, including information on admission fees, parking and/or public transportation information, and a pamphlet about the location's exhibits, will support parents in planning a follow-up visit of their own. If a location has special family programming or discounted admission days, this information will also be helpful to include.

SPECIAL CONSIDERATIONS: STUDENTS RECEIVING SPECIAL EDUCATION SERVICES

There are thousands of students in the United States who receive special education services (Heward & Orlansky, 1992). Some are mainstreamed full time within a regular education classroom. Others may be placed within a self-contained special education class and join the regular education classroom for select programs depending on a student's Individualized Education Plan (IEP). Whatever a student's placement, students with disabilities will benefit tremendously from field trip experiences, perhaps even more than their regular education peers (see Student Story B).

For example, students with low vision often find that the hands-on nature of many field trips provides unique touching experiences impossible in a traditional classroom. Students with physical impairments may find the open spaces and large galleries a welcoming place to learn without having to maneuver within a traditionally tight classroom space. Students with cognitive delays may find that the authentic context and realia to be helpful in comprehending abstract concepts about art or historical theory. A student with processing difficulties may find that a field trip's reinforcement of the classroom curriculum really helps with retention. Students with attentional disorders may find comfort in being able to explore and learn kinesthetically, with a range of engaging exhibits to hold their interest. Those with multiple involvements who might be working on personal and social goals will receive important experience in navigating public spaces.

Whatever a student's disability, a field trip experience can significantly support development of cognitive and social goals. However, sometimes special planning and accommodations are necessary to tap fully into a special education student's strengths and create a positive visit experience.

Tip 1: Offering an Invitation

For students receiving special education services mainstreamed within another classroom for any part of the day, it is important to extend an invitation to take part in upcoming field trips through the child's special education teacher. The two teachers can then work together to determine who will coordinate getting the permission slip signed by the child's parent or guardian.

It is also helpful to consider extending an invite to a child who is not mainstreamed into the regular education classroom, but is at the same grade level as those students. Field trips may be difficult for a special education teacher within a self-contained classroom to conduct with a wide range of grade levels and specialized services to juggle. Including his or her students in already established field trip plans will be much appreciated.

Some classroom teachers may hesitate to include students with physical disabilities, not out of a desire for exclusion but purely out of concern for a student's physical safety in an area that may not be entirely accessible. This is a valid concern and one worthy of conversation. However, the decision to accompany the class or not due to safety concerns should rest with the child and his or her family. Often, families may have helpful experiences with overcoming limited access, and will know how to make a potentially challenging trip a possibility.

Tip 2: Prepare for the Visit

If you will be bringing a student with special needs, speak briefly with the parents about any special considerations for an off-site trip. Some things that are not a problem within a classroom environment may take a little extra effort during an off-site visit. If the child is not part of your regular classroom, have a brief talk with the child's special education teacher. He or she will be aware of the child's academic goals, cognitive or physical limitations, and any behavioral problems and can help prepare for the trip. It is important to make this contact well in advance of the trip so there is time to get permission slips signed as well as potentially arrange for the special education paraprofessional to accompany the student if necessary.

In addition, check with the school office well ahead of the field trip to determine if any students will require medication during the school day. Lead time will be needed to complete any necessary paperwork and arrange for storage and administration of the medication while off site.

Tip 3: Contact the Site

It will also be important to contact the field trip site ahead of time to confirm that it is fully accessible and safe, as well as to identify the most appropriate entrances, amenities, and parking facilities to use. Many locations have family restrooms that provide both space and privacy for a student who may require the help of a personal care assistant to use the restroom. If this student is a part of your regular classroom, you may already have an idea of what his or her special needs are. If not, be sure to speak with the parents and/or special education teacher.

While planning for accessibility concerns, beware of circumstances that may be logistically convenient but create situations that highlight the disability of the student and may create feelings of discomfort. For example, if the accessible entrance is not the traditional school-visit entrance, rather than sending only the student with physical disabilities to that entrance, ask if all students can enter together.

The National Arts and Disability Center provides information to museums about creating spaces that are universally accessible. By reviewing these resources, you can make an informed decision in selecting a universally accessible site for your school field trip.

Tip 4: During the Visit Details

It is common to group students during a field trip. Be sure to partner students with special needs with peers who will be helpful and encouraging yet still allow them to think and act on their own. Sometimes peers are so eager to help, they may overlook the many abilities of a student with special needs. Create an on-site activity that is indeed within the student's capabilities and then simply instruct peers to help only if the student requests assistance. Be aware that you may need to make some modifications or provide additional support to students with special needs.

Tip 5: Following Up

If students from another classroom have been included and there is a special follow-up project, be sure to invite student participation and provide the special education teacher details. An additional option is to send home a brief note outlining the exciting things that happened on the field trip and suggestions for follow-up at home. Some students with special needs may have cognitive delays or communication disorders that might make communicating the details of the trip difficult. A note gives parents a jump start to talking to their child about the adventure.

UNIVERSAL ACCESS AND MUSEUMS

In recent years, museums and other informal learning institutions have been working very hard to create exhibitions and visitor experiences that are relevant to a diverse visitorship—whatever their primary language and in spite of a disability. Contacting your field trip destination ahead of time will help you plan for the many different resources that make these locations relevant to a diverse visitorship.

Helpful Web Sites

These Web sites provide information on the legal responsibilities of museums in providing universal access as well as information on how exhibits and museum experiences can be structured to provide universal access.

Association of Science-Technology Centers: Accessible Practices
Resource Center
http://astc.org/resource/access

National Arts and Disability Center
http://www.nadc.ucla.edu/about.cfm

National Endowment for the Arts: Office for AccessAbility
http://www.nea.gov/resources/Accessibility/index.html

Student Story A

Monica Kohlbatz shares her childhood experiences with field trips as an English learner.

"As an English language learner, having the opportunity to go on a field trip helped me further develop and reinforce my English skills. Interacting with peers in a less stressful environment motivated me to participate more in class discussions. Furthermore, the field trip provided me with the chance to take what I had learned in the classroom and apply it out in the field. I feel that this experience increased my self-esteem and gave me the confidence that I needed to succeed as a student."

Student Story B

Josh Niklason uses a manual wheelchair. When asked to reflect on his experiences with field trips, he had both positive memories and reflections on situations that he wish had been handled differently.

"At the surface, my field trip experiences were positive, but behind the scenes there were more negative aspects to the experience than I initially realized. On the positive side, I was always able to attend the field trips. I feel the field trips really benefited me because I learn best visually and hands-on. A field trip is a perfect example of that form of learning. There were some things I wish could have been done differently. I appreciate that the teachers and my fellow students tried to be accommodating. However, several things set me apart from my peers. My parent usually had to struggle with the school to order a separate, more accommodating school bus or I would have to ride in my parents' car.

The fact that my parent had to come with me so I could travel with my wheelchair set me apart, too. Many times I would travel on the separate bus alone or with only a few random students. I would have liked it if the teachers were at least more discrete with the issue of other students riding with me. I believe the ideal thing would have been to ask me how I wanted the situation to be handled. Towards the end of elementary, I couldn't attend many major field trips for medical problems. Since I was in the hospital for roughly half of the school year, I understand that rescheduling these trips was not an option. It would have been nice if I had been informed of the in-class activities leading up to the field trip instead of only work related to my academic learning."

8

Technically Speaking

Using Technology to Enhance Field Trips

Many educators are already aware of the different ways technology can support, enhance, or even replace traditional field trips. Taking a "virtual tour" of a field trip destination is something a number of educators have already infused into the curriculum. Many more know to check a destination's Web site for helpful information. However, there are many additional ways technology can support a field trip visit or serve as an alternative experience when a trip is not possible (Cox-Petersen & Melber, 2001).

All of these suggestions are made in line with the National Education Technology Standards (International Society for Educational Technology, 1998), specifically the following:

- Standard 3: Technology Productivity Tools
- Standard 4: Technology Communications Tools
- Standard 5: Technology Research Tools
- Standard 6: Technology Problem-Solving and Decision Making Tools

SUPPORTING A VISIT

Internet Connections

1. Spend time browsing a field trip destination's Web site prior to the visit. The very basic use of this source should be to download maps and exhibit information. Both teachers and students can use this information to guide the structure of the visit.

2. Spend time reviewing the Web site for content information or suggested activities that can help build student understanding before the visit.

Many sites have field trip tips, downloadable curriculum guides, or multimedia offerings to prepare students for the many things they will encounter on their trip.

3. Take note of any special programs on the day of the visit. If necessary, call ahead to ensure participation if there is a limit to the number of students the program can serve.

Word Processing

1. Compile student-friendly field guides with images and words that will help them navigate the field trip destination. These can be laminated for durability or attached to a clipboard.

2. Design name tags quickly using printer-friendly labels.

3. Create activity sheets or student journals that can be used during the on-site investigations. Because exhibits change frequently, be sure to confirm that any activity sheets are consistent with current offerings through a pretrip visit or Internet search.

4. Draft a letter to parents outlining the visit goals and optional follow-up activities that can be conducted at home.

5. Create a newsletter or bulletin board upon return, sharing class discoveries with the rest of the school.

Digital Camera (Still/Video)

1. Document students actively engaged in field trip activities. These can be printed and stored in student portfolios for later assessment.

2. Capture images of exhibits, animals, or artifacts that students find especially interesting for later study. For example, photograph something for a later project, report, or presentation.

3. Take photos of the visit to use as preparation for student visits in subsequent years.

4. Burn images or video onto individual CD-ROMs for students to keep as a souvenir of the visit.

Note: Field trip destinations may have regulations regarding the taking of photographs. Many will not allow flash photography. Check with the destination before designing activities to ensure that visit plans are in line with regulations.

PRESENTATION SOFTWARE

1. Create a multimedia summary of the trip and any associated projects for display on a school Web site. Multimedia presentations can include video clips, sound clips, narrative text, and digital images.

2. Create a multimedia documentation of the trip and associated activities to share at a school open house or other parent evening.

TECHNOLOGY ALTERNATIVES

Sometimes a field trip can simply not be arranged. Technology offers several alternative pathways for students to tap into the content and expertise of relevant institutions from the comfort of the classroom.

Consult With Experts

One of the greatest assets of a museum or other field trip destination is the presence of world-renowned experts. Internet Webcams and e-mail access can help a classroom teacher tap into the expertise of these professionals without a physical visit. There are many Web sites that allow students to "Ask an Expert," and these can be wonderful resources. However, many experts find they are often overwhelmed with questions and can post responses to only a few frequently asked questions. Rather than approaching a consultation with an expert as a one-shot question-and-answer session, it is helpful to form a connection with someone who can support the classroom curriculum in a number of ways.

The best way to identify an expert for personalized consultations is networking through friends and family. The benefit of e-mail correspondence is that there are no geographical limits. Even a second cousin living three thousand miles away is a viable option. After possible partners have been identified, determine through e-mail what they might be available to help with. Are they willing to answer questions that cannot be solved through library research? Are they interested in providing career guidance? Would they be willing to send photos of themselves conducting research or otherwise performing their work responsibilities? In addition to e-mail correspondence, Webcasts are another option.

Webcasts provide student access to an expert who might not have time for personalized correspondence (Bell, 2003). Many institutions archive footage from live Webcasts so you can access the information at a time convenient for you and your students. Some researchers will conduct Webcasts from around the world to update the public on their research and provide students with an in-depth view of what research is like. Podcasts are another option to consider. They are often shorter in duration and can be sent via e-mail.

Internet blogs or diaries that track the work of an expert on a daily basis can be rich resources for students. Of course, it is important to review the site and ensure the entries are professionally related and appropriate for students. However, it is the personal (though still age-appropriate) touches, such as complaints about travel glitches or project-specific difficulties, that help students understand the human side of the work of a professional mathematician, librarian, or scientific researcher.

Helpful Web Sites

These sites offer archived and real-time Webcasts that address concepts in science, math, social science, the arts, and literacy.

The Field Museum: Expeditions
http://www.fieldmuseum.org/expeditions

Library of Congress: Webcasts
http://www.libraryofcongress.gov/today/cyberlc

University of North Carolina: Webcasts
http://www.unctv.org/webcast

Access Collections

A visit to a field trip site is special because it can provide access to objects and experiences not available on school grounds. However, many people do not know that the large majority of an institution's collections and treasures may not be on exhibit. These collections are housed in nonpublic spaces where researchers study them and protect them from damage. Even libraries keep the rarest manuscripts and books off the floor. Zoos and aquariums have "collections." They refer to the plants and animals they care for as "living collections" (American Zoological Association, 2006) that must be appropriately cared for and conserved.

By using the Internet, students can access these protected collections through searchable, online databases. These databases provide students with the means to

- investigate weaving patterns from a variety of Navajo blankets.
- view an animal-cam and take scientific notes about animal behavior.
- compare paintings by the same artist over several different years.
- read a personal diary dating back to the 1700s.
- compare the sizes of different types of sharks.

Some regional field trip destinations even provide online field guides to help students identify the plants and animals they might find around the schoolyard.

Helpful Web Sites

These Web sites provide searchable Internet access to collections.

Art Institute of Chicago
http://www.artic.edu/aic/collections

California Academy of the Sciences: Anthropology
http://www.calacademy.org/research/anthropology

Cornell University Library: Division of Rare and Manuscript Collection
http://rmc.library.cornell.edu

Library of Congress: Rare Book and Special Collections Reading Room
http://www.libraryofcongress.gov/rr/rarebook

Monterey Bay Aquarium: Live Webcams
http://www.mbayaq.org/efc/cam_menu.asp

National Museum of American History
http://americanhistory.si.edu/collections

National Zoo: Animal Cams
http://nationalzoo.si.edu/animals/webcams

Smithsonian National Museum of Natural History
http://www.mnh.si.edu/rc

NEW HORIZONS

The suggestions provided here can be implemented at almost any field trip destination. However, exciting new technologies are being incorporated at informal learning institutions around the nation. This may include podcasts in conjunction with special exhibits, or the technology to link a personal data assistant (PDA) to download the latest video clips and images during a visit (Marcotte, 2006). A unique challenge may be to explore the use of laptops within exhibitions or during investigations at a local park. Local businesses might be willing to demonstrate how technology supports their everyday logistics as well as break new ground such as "virtually" changing wall color on a computer screen before selecting a new hue. Thinking outside the box when planning a field trip—be it virtual or actual—and incorporating technology in a variety of ways is an important step toward making quality connections.

9

Making Your Case

Information to Share With Administrators

I t is true that field trips have been an important part of the school experience for decades. However, as school budgets have dwindled, transportation costs skyrocketed, and high-stakes testing has become more prominent, teachers may find it takes a little extra planning and convincing in order to get a field trip approved.

Most school districts have basic procedures in place for arranging and organizing a field trip. This chapter does not review district-specific request procedures, but rather presents a theoretical framework for supporting the importance of a field trip. Being able to communicate how field trips can have a significant impact in direct support of the classroom curriculum is the best way to ensure a "green light" for the planned excursion. What follows is information that can help in addressing some common administrative concerns.

"We have such a rich curriculum to cover, we don't have time for extras like field trips."

Field trips should not be considered extras but rather a significant part of the curriculum, critical to a true understanding of complex concepts. The work of educational researchers as well as professional groups supports this stance. For example:

- John Dewey (1938) states that firsthand experiences are crucial to learning new concepts as well as positioning the learner for future educational experiences.

- Howard Gardner (1991) specifically states the importance of connecting schools and museums to support student learning and accommodate different learning styles.
- The National Research Council (1999) asserts the importance of first-hand experience in brain development and later learning, specifically noting the importance of quality connections to community resources such as local business and museums.
- A number of national curriculum organizations cite field trips as a critical component of a quality curriculum. These include
  - National Council for the Social Studies (1993)
  - National Council of Teachers of Mathematics (2000)
  - National Science Teachers Association (1998)

As we strive for an inclusive curriculum (U.S. Department of Education, 2004), tapping into field trip destinations can provide the resources necessary to support a truly experiential approach to curriculum.

"Our English learners really need to be focusing on building fluency right now—field trips will need to wait."

It is clear that varied teaching methods are critical to working effectively with a student body that is becoming increasingly diverse culturally and linguistically. One of the most effective ways to support these students in content knowledge is providing real-world context (Watson & Houtz, 2003). A field trip provides this context and allows students to engage with the content in an authentic setting. These object-rich experiences are especially helpful in vocabulary building (Lapp, Fisher, & Flood, 1999), particularly with vocabulary words that may have more than one meaning (Rule & Barrera, 2003).

"We have very limited funds. Can't we just create a similar experience in the classroom?"

Whatever the busing costs or admission fees that have been requested for a field trip, it will be considerably less expensive than trying to re-create these same experiences within a classroom environment. In addition, a carefully chosen field trip destination will focus on a location that offers something that cannot be explored in a classroom setting, such as a unique work of art, a rare plant, or an antique artifact. When was the last time there was a panda roaming the school hallway or a Picasso hanging in the school library?

While there are certainly bus fees associated with visits to informal learning sites, it is important to realize that over half of the nation's museums have free admission and many more offer a particular day that is free of charge (American Association of Museums, 2006). Further, many museums that do have regular admission fees will often waive these for visiting school groups. It is often possible to avoid bus fees by selecting a field trip site within walking distance of the school.

"We need all our activities to be standards-focused—field trips just don't fit into that."

A carefully chosen destination will easily meet required curriculum standards. In fact, many museums specifically structure their programs around state standards in math, science, fine arts, or history (American Association of Museums, 2006). However, sometimes an administrator just needs some quick proof of this. It is a good idea to prepare a short summary of the trip's objectives and the standards that the field trip activities will address. Some field trip destinations might have literature that identifies the different standards that their programs and exhibits focus on. This book also indicates national standards that can be met through the different suggested activities.

"This year we are focusing only on activities that will improve student performance on standardized tests."

It is important to make the test-centric administrator aware of research indicating that student engagement in inquiry-based learning with real objects and specimens can support learning associated with content on standardized tests (Klentschy, 2002; Stohr-Hunt, 1996; Wenglinsky, 2000; Wise, 1996), particularly for students from culturally and linguistically diverse backgrounds. If this information does not help sway an administrator, another option is to suggest the trip take place after the high-stakes testing period or at the beginning of the school year, when preparation for testing has not yet reached full emphasis.

"How does taking a field trip fit with No Child Left Behind?"

No Child Left Behind is focused on providing a quality education for all students and providing access to learning resources to every child regardless of their income level or background (U.S. Department of Education, 2004). For many students, the school-sponsored field trip may be their only exposure to real-world context, critical for reinforcement of content learned strictly from books.

In addition, No Child Left Behind focuses on the importance of highly qualified teachers (U.S. Department of Education, 2004). However, even the most highly trained educator will likely not simultaneously carry the expertise of a librarian, mathematician, research scientist, and art curator. Visits to field trip sites give access to "specialty educators" who can provide a unique learning experience for students.

"Students can get out of control on field trips. We need them focused on learning right now."

True. Sometimes students can get very excited on a field trip and thus raise concerns that learning has taken a backseat to having fun. However, research indicates that when a learner can focus on a topic of personal interest and excitement, more significant learning gains can be observed (Covington, 1998). Experiences with subjects that are enjoyable and engaging, such as the arts, are especially critical for at-risk students, who can go on to make connections to additional curricular areas (Diket, 2003).

So while running crazy should not be tolerated, "having fun" can have some significant cognitive gains that should not be disregarded. That is where the carefully planned on-site activity comes in. Demonstrating to an administrator that there is a focused agenda for the visit will assuage visions of students hanging from balconies and running from exhibit to exhibit.

LAST WORDS

When communicating with a headmaster or principal, it is important to treat the field trip request as a business proposal that demonstrates professional planning and expertise (see Figure 9.1 for an example). Include necessary figures that reflect the total cost of the trip. It is also a good idea to explain the special on-site project that students will be conducting so administrators can see how the unique attributes of the field trip site are being utilized. In addition, if the first choice for a field trip is too expensive, it will be helpful to plan for a second, less expensive option. For example, a local aquarium might have an entry fee that is outside the school's budget. However, an appropriate alternative might be a trip to the local shoreline or tidepool area, with no admission fee.

If the school district absolutely does not have funding for field trips, consider looking to other sources for funding. Though identifying specific funders with national relevance is beyond the scope of this book, here are some general tips that can help in finding a funder to match your field trip needs.

- Foundations that support field trips are usually regional, so start the funding search close to home. One option is to start with the venue itself and see if they have grants for transportation.
- Conduct an online search using key terms "field trip grants" together with the city or county name. Funders that offer smaller grants of $1,000 or under will be the best match for a one-time field trip request.
- Some districts have parent-led educational foundations that might also be a good place to request field trip funding.
- Consider contacting the head office of local corporations. Markets, banks, and even department stores often have small grant programs targeted to schools in the area where they do the most of their business.

Figure 9.1   Proposed Field Trip to the Ramsey Historic Home

Request

The fourth-grade teachers would like to arrange a field trip to the local Ramsey Historic Home to support their studies in the areas of social science, science, and language arts.

Ramsey Historic Home

This historic farmhouse highlights life during the 1800s here in our own town. The home is filled with antiques and historic artifacts to help students gain a better understanding of early lifeways. There is a petting zoo comprised of the animals that would have been found on early farms, as well as a historically accurate garden. There are several interpreters who dress in period costume and assume the role of different members of the Ramsey family.

Cost

> 2 Buses: $350 each (8 A.M.–1 P.M.)
> Admission: $1/student = $60 (teachers and chaperones are free)
> Optional Cost: $.50/student to touch farm animals in the petting zoo
> Total Cost: $760 (no petting zoo visit)
> $790 (with petting zoo visit)

On-Site Project

Students will be conducting a research study of historic artifacts and design to compare with a field study of their own homes. During our visit, they will be taking photographs (as permitted by the conservancy), taking notes on the different antique artifacts on display, and interviewing the educational interpreters for information on the Ramsey family. All of this data will be compiled in our "now and then" projects, which will be on display during the fourth-grade history fair.

National Standards Links

Note: Some districts may want to see state as well as national standards here.

Social Science (National Council for the Social Studies, 1994)

- Theme 2: Time, Continuity, and Change
- Theme 4: Individual Development and Identity
- Theme 5: Individuals, Groups, and Institutions

Science (National Research Council, 1996):

- Standard C: Life Science

Different species of farm animals and the historic garden will allow for life science studies.

Language Arts (National Council of Teachers of English & International Reading Association, 1996)

- Standard 7: Students conduct research on issues and interests.

Evaluation of Visit

Students will be required to complete a field notebook during their visit focused on the data they will need in order to complete their final project. Student notebooks will be continually monitored during the visit to ensure students are staying focused and on task.

10

When You Have to Stay on Campus

Alternatives to Off-Site Field Trips

Unfortunately, there are many factors that can make taking a field trip with students impossible. Sometimes budget concerns are the culprit. Other times the field trip site may be sold out. Maybe the school is located in a rural area far from larger museums, galleries, or even a corner grocery store. Or perhaps the allotted field trip for the year has already been taken. Whatever the reason, it is important to note that a carefully planned on-site "field trip" can be a great alternative to an off-site excursion.

GENERAL TIPS FOR ALTERNATIVE FIELD TRIP ACTIVITIES

It will still be important to incorporate extra planning to create a quality on-site experience. These general tips will help any activity run smoothly.

Replicate the Process Rather Than Just the Content

What makes field trips so special to students is the opportunity to *see* and *do* something. It is this active involvement in addition to content gains that makes a field trip so influential. When designing an alternative field trip activity, consider the use of authentic objects and specimens, opportunities for touching, exploration of a novel phenomenon, or interaction with a guest expert.

Arrange for Permission

Be sure to check with the principal about any special plan. If the plan is to use the schoolyard, it will be important to make sure students do not end up in the middle of someone else's PE class. If the choice is to walk students to a neighboring field or wooded area, this most likely will require a parental permission slip. Whatever the plan, be sure there is permission in line to take students where they need to go.

Show Excitement

When the teacher shows the same excitement for a special activity as an off-site field trip, students will feel the same way. Create name tags, initiate a countdown before the special day to help build anticipation, or leave a special note on the door alerting visitors where the class has disappeared to.

Integrate Novelty

While research indicates that too much novelty can detract from student learning, a small amount can enhance cognitive gains. Most of us have felt a sense of excitement when faced with something new and how that excitement can more effectively draw us into the learning experience. In order to generate high energy on the part of students, an alternative activity will need to be distinct from what might happen every day in the classroom. Whatever the choice, be sure to incorporate something students have never seen before: a strange plant, a new individual, or even a part of the schoolyard usually off limits.

Involve Parents

One drawback of a traditional field trip is that there may be limits on the number of parents that can come along due to bus space or admission fees. Take advantage of an on-site plan to include as much parental participation as possible.

Alert the Media

Though one drawback of a smaller or rural location may be access to city museums, one of the many advantages is often a very supportive community. Invite the local media to cover a special project as a human interest piece. How many traditional field trips end up in the newspaper?

FIELD TRIP ALTERNATIVES

The following projects are not arranged by curricular area. These activities are integrated across the curriculum and can also easily be modified to emphasize one curriculum area over another, depending on teaching needs.

Object Investigation

Many of the activities described in the preceding chapters focused on interaction with authentic objects and specimens. While it is true that a field trip site will have unique objects not accessible anywhere else, museum-quality objects are not necessary to create a similar investigation activity in the classroom.

A quick inventory of home and backyard will most likely turn up a number of potential objects. Grandparents or other extended family members are another source for unique and historic items. Local garage sales or discount stores are also excellent sources. If there is extra funding, a number of companies can supply objects and artifacts for use in the classroom. A quick Internet search will easily provide you with a number of choices.

The main objective of artifact investigation is to encourage active inquiry on the part of students as well as the authentic use of language arts and math skills in context to convey understanding. Even a simple object such as a flower to dissect, money from another country, or an antique button can serve as the focal point of this observation (see the vignette at the end of this chapter).

Ecological Field Investigations

There is no need to travel to a zoo or botanical garden to conduct field studies of nature and ecology. Any outdoor space, from an urban schoolyard to acres of woods, can serve as a study site for students. The benefit of conducting these investigations in the schoolyard over a field trip site is that there can be repeated investigations, just as a real scientist would conduct, throughout the school year. Following are some investigation projects for consideration.

- Track the weather daily and create a class graph to summarize the data. Have older students record daily temperature or rainfall measures.
- Start a school bird feeder project and keep track of the types of birds the feeder attracts.
- Go on an arthropod hunt around the schoolyard. Which areas attract the most critters?
- Conduct a vegetation survey, identifying the species that are most common as well as species that are found in only one or two places.

Classroom Museum

Just because students cannot make it to a museum does not mean the experience cannot be replicated on school grounds. Students might create an art museum through the use of inexpensive prints designed for teachers, computer printouts of famous paintings from online resources, or even works of art by local artists. Another option is to conduct a sweep of the neighborhood, asking to borrow (nonvaluable) antiques or photocopies of historic photos to create a mini-museum of local history. Another choice is to take up a collection from the faculty at school and order a collection of skulls, furs, antlers, and other scientific specimens to make a school-based natural history museum. Some field trip destinations even have loan programs allowing educators to check out unique objects for classroom use.

However students gather objects, the next step is to "interpret" them with simple labels and find an area to display them. One option is to ask if students can borrow a section of the school library. To create a mini-museum on a larger scale, students may turn to the school auditorium and invite a number of other teachers and students to participate. Once the mini-museum is created, any of the activities described in the preceding chapters can be implemented.

For a truly integrated learning experience, create a mini-museum where students take the lead. When students take the lead using objects that are important to them, the learning experience is greatly enhanced (Cox-Petersen & Melber, 1999). From selecting a special object or artifact they would like to display to writing the label, the actual design, and creation of an exhibit, all areas of the curriculum are covered in this project. Students will need to rely on measurement skills to design the actual exhibit and language arts skills to create a perfect exhibit label as well as an exhibit guide.

ADDITIONAL OPTIONS

Tap Into Local Businesses

Several types of businesses are referenced throughout this book as locations to explore specific areas of the curriculum. Take a look around the school neighborhood and think creatively about how a local business could turn into a fantastic walking field trip. Perhaps a locally owned market in your community would allow students to practice the process of making change. Maybe an enterprise that does most of its business by mail will allow students to tally and graph where the packages are being delivered as a lesson on U.S. geography.

Invite an Expert

When it is not possible to get to the professional, invite the professional to come to the class! The key to convincing a busy individual to visit a classroom is to demonstrate planning as well as a true understanding of the individual's field. Creating a unique and creative request, carefully tied to the curriculum and the guest speaker's expertise, is critical. For example, while learning about the importance of laws to a society, you may want to design a mock trial for students. When they are well prepared to take part in the trial, invite a local attorney to be the guest judge. After the presentation, you can provide time for the attorney to discuss how the re-creation was similar to or different from an actual trial.

Not sure where to track down an expert? One way to locate potential speakers is through parents. You might want to ask each parent to suggest three potential visitors to the classroom—that could result in over sixty suggestions! Local colleges and universities are another source of professionals with diverse areas of expertise. Look into conferences or expos that might be coming to the local area and see who will be attending. This can be one way to get a visit by an expert that normally would be out of reach. A final option is to identify a Webcast by an expert in line with your classroom studies (Bell, 2003).

Try Technology

One of the easiest ways to expand the walls of the classroom without leaving it is through technology. There are a number of different activities you can do with technology that parallel on-site field trip activities (Marcotte, 2006) and will not require bus reservations. Conducting a virtual field trip, "visiting" a museum, zoo, park, or gallery on-line through the use of the Internet, is perhaps the most common way that teachers use technology to expand the learning horizons of their students. Chapter 8 explores additional methods of incorporating technology for quality experiences both on site and off site.

CONCLUSION

Though field trip experiences definitely provide a certain magic of their own, it is not impossible to create equally dynamic and engaging activities within the constraints of the classroom and neighboring schoolyard. When the focus is on active learning and connection to authentic experiences, a "field trip" can take place almost anywhere.

Vignette: Object Investigation

"This is the artifact I'm going to use for my research journal!" fourth grader Marisela announces as she plunks herself down in front of a table with touchable yet unidentified artifacts. She takes out a small packet of folded paper and begins to write a brief description of what she sees.

"That is an interesting piece," Ms. Nguyen responds as she does a quick head count of the other students just a couple of feet away. "What are you discovering through your observations?"

"It looks like it's made of metal. But the metal isn't shiny any more, so I think it's kinda old."

"It does look old. What can you tell me about its shape?"

Marisela begins to speak but is cut off by an eager classmate. "It's a railroad tie. I saw one at my grandpa's house," offers Sean, who is working with an object next to Marisela.

Marisela sends him a crushed look reserved for people who routinely ruin surprises. "I guess you're right," she remarks and starts to skip to the bottom of the page reserved for her "preliminary conclusions."

Ms. Nguyen gently encourages Sean to focus on his artifact and leans in closer to Marisela. "Let's not skip steps here. I agree with Sean that it does look a little like a railroad tie, but it seems a little small to hold down a track for such a huge train. Let's finish our description and look at the other things on the table here."

Marisela squints at the tie and at her research journal. She completes the different sections asking her to measure the object, describe its shape and color, and indicate what type of social science researcher she thinks would be most helpful to contact in order to learn more. When she reaches the section focused on tapping into her prior knowledge, she remembers the chapter they just read in their social studies books on "Life in the Mines."

"Didn't they have mini-railroads to get coal and gold and stuff out of mines?!" Marisela shouts to her teacher, who has moved away to guide another student. Her teacher answers with a thumbs-up and a smile, and Marisela excitedly bends over her research journal to record her findings.

11

Learning for You

*Teacher Resources
at Informal Learning Sites*

I nformal learning institutions are not simply learning resources for students. Educators can also find a wealth of information to augment their classroom teaching, provide growth in content knowledge, and deliver community service opportunities. This chapter summarizes just a few of the many opportunities that await educators.

FREE AND LOW-COST MATERIALS

Many informal learning institutions have materials for educators to help make your field trip experience run more smoothly and extend the experience into the classroom. Some institutions have standards-linked curriculum guides to enhance classroom instruction. These are often available free of charge from institutions' Web sites, or may be available for a nominal fee in hard copy format.

Other institutions have specimen or artifact loan programs that function like object libraries. These services provide access to specimens and artifacts that lack the necessary background data important for research. For this reason the items have been set aside for educational use—by museum educators and sometimes even classroom teachers. Items from colonial artifacts to a taxidermied eagle to a comprehensive collection of art prints are often transferred to education departments for use in educating the public on the work of researchers.

EDUCATOR WORKSHOPS AND COURSES

Field trip sites that are valuable learning experiences for students can also support professional growth. Many informal learning institutions have programs for teachers as well as students. These might be one-day workshops or online courses lasting several months. Whatever the preferred format, there is sure to be a course that matches even the busiest teacher's schedule.

The benefits of attending professional development training at a field trip destination are considerable. It provides educators with access to the latest information in the field. Our understanding of learning and the world around us is changing so quickly, books can become outdated just weeks after publication. Informal learning sites may also provide access to experts who may be difficult to connect with in any other situation. These programs often include access to and interaction with the specimens, animals, artifacts, and works of art that are the institution's unique holdings. This creates an experiential learning opportunity that not only is engaging, but also helps with retention of content. In short, such programs model precisely the type of experience important to create for students as part of a field trip or partnership opportunity.

Programs and offerings vary by field trip site and may change from year to year depending on funding or institutional priorities. The best way to find the most appropriate workshop or course is to visit the Web sites of locations within the community to see what is being offered. Journals and newsletters published by professional organizations often advertise distance learning courses appropriate to a particular area of the curriculum and connected to institutions that lie outside the community.

SEASONAL EMPLOYMENT

Some field trip destinations have a need for seasonal employees. This may present a good opportunity for an educator on break. Many educators enjoy part-time work during school vacations to augment salaries or to cultivate a new skill base. These might include teaching within summer camp programs, office work during a busy season, additional help in greeting and guiding visitors, or even writing curriculum. If a first try at seasonal employment within these institutions is not successful, it is important not to get discouraged. Volunteering can be a first step in getting to know the staff and the institution and may lead to seasonal employment at a later date. Working for an informal institution can provide valuable insights into different methods of instruction as well as contacts that may support the classroom curriculum at a later date.

VOLUNTEER OPPORTUNITIES

Many teachers have chunks of time away from the classroom, such as winter recess or summer break. While most teachers need this time to catch their breath and prepare for resumption of classes, some also like to use this time to volunteer within their community or take part in activities to enhance their own teaching. Informal learning institutions such as museums often have unique volunteer opportunities that cannot be found anywhere else.

Most informal learning institutions rely heavily on volunteers to keep things running smoothly. A natural history museum may rely on volunteers to help catalog specimens. A wildlife rehabilitation facility may need volunteers to help clean cages. An art museum may need someone to help stuff envelopes for their annual fundraiser or greet visitors as they enter the event. Some may even want to train educators to serve as interpreters during times of heavy visitation. While not all volunteer positions at these locations will be glamorous, being connected can provide unique opportunities. It can be a chance to stretch knowledge in a particular subject or engage with artifacts or objects not accessible to the general public.

Volunteers can also make connections that might benefit students at a later date. For example, a researcher for whom a teacher made hundreds of photocopies might be more easily persuaded to visit a class of third graders in the fall. The best way to find a good volunteer match for your schedule and area of interest is simply to contact the institution directly.

SAMPLE RESOURCES

Many programs and resources for educators change from year to year depending on available funding, educator interest, and national standards trends. Below are a few samples of professional development programs and educator resources available in each of the five curricular areas covered in this book and valid at press time. However, be sure to link with your regional institution in order to identify even more opportunities to get connected.

Social Science

Earthwatch Educator Fellowships

Earthwatch provides opportunities for the public to volunteer alongside social science (and science) researchers in the field as they conduct research all over the world. Participating is fee-based, but there are a number of fellowships available to educators, students, and administrators to cover or offset expedition costs. Graduate-level credit is also available and participation can be arranged during school vacations.
http://www.earthwatch.org

Science

American Museum of Natural History: Online Courses

AMNH offers online courses for educators in a variety of science content areas. Graduate credit is available and the program is affiliated with the National Science Teacher Association.
http://education.amnh.org

Math

The Exploratorium: Math Explorer Online Lessons

The Exploratorium provides free activity ideas for educators, connected to a variety of mathematical concepts. The Web site contains a searchable database to identify the activity that best matches a particular mathematical concept and learning modality.
http://www.exploratorium.edu/math_explorer/

Fine Arts

National Gallery of Art: Loan Program

This program allows teachers nationwide to borrow videos, slide programs, and other curricular items to support art instruction in the classroom.
http://www.nga.gov/education/classroom/loanfinder

Language Arts

Smithsonian Education: Language Arts Resources

This site has a searchable database covering all topics. The page dedicated to language arts supports educators with the integration of language arts into museum-related activities.
http://www.smithsonianeducation.org/educators

CONCLUSION

Informal learning institutions are not simply resources for the elementary student. They can provide free or low-cost curriculum resources and professional development opportunities for educators as well. Whether you take advantage of those closest to your community or online offerings, informal learning sites can offer significant support for the classroom curriculum.

Conclusion

Field trips can be the highlight of the school year. They are not only a chance for students to explore a world outside the school grounds but also an opportunity to breathe life into the classroom curriculum. Every day, teachers around the nation are discovering just how successful a well-planned field trip can be, both academically and emotionally. Perhaps the best way to conclude this work is to leave the reader with a vignette from a recent field trip organized by Colleen Kessler, a third-grade teacher from Ohio.

Vignette: A Visit to Hale Farm and Village

For Mrs. Kessler, a visit to the nearby Hale Farm and Village was the perfect field trip. A component of the Western Reserve Historical Society, Hale Farm and Village is a working farm complete with an adjoining town highlighting ways of life in our recent past. As part of their social studies curriculum, her third-grade students were studying pioneers as well as the movement of goods and services through a community. Mrs. Kessler was also excited to include science in the trip: their classroom unit on simple machines would be an excellent match for the farm equipment they would encounter during their visit.

With only one or two field trips allotted per year, Mrs. Kessler wanted to make the most of this visit. She planned their trip to coincide with a special Harvest Festival, when there would be even more historical reenactments and activities in which students could participate. The advance planning also made it easy to procure enough parent chaperones and prepare them to assist with the students' learning tasks.

The visit provided students with the opportunity to watch artisans—glassblowers, candle makers, basket weavers, and potters—take raw materials and turn them into consumer goods. In addition, students were asked to participate in the different farming activities and chore re-creations. They struggled to help the "farmer's wife" churn butter and left that activity with a huge appreciation for the dairy aisle of the local supermarket. The girls enjoyed handling the fancy crinoline and other early garments but commented on their preference for jeans when they realized how long it took just to get dressed back then. As it was harvest time, there were very real farming duties that students could help with. They picked and shucked corn, and even helped with harvesting the vegetables—quickly learning just what it entailed to keep a farm running.

During the visit, students were asked to serve as documentary historians as well as active participants, using a disposable camera to make a record of themselves and their peers taking part in the different chores. This translated into a postvisit activity as well.

(Continued)

135

(Continued)

Back in the classroom, students continued to use the disposable camera over the next few weeks to document themselves at work in their own homes, taking part in everyday chores of today. Students later compiled the images and written explanations into a scrapbook, comparing and contrasting their lives today with life in the past, in line with national standards.

Mrs. Kessler comments that one of the most exciting outcomes of the field trip was the students' deeper understanding of what things they had in common with children from the past, as well as the new discoveries and technologies that have provided us with everyday conveniences. Perhaps the favorite part of the trip for the parent chaperones was hearing students murmuring on the bus about liking their chores at home much better than the physically taxing farm work! This was a field trip that was talked about for a long time afterward—by students, parents, and teachers alike.

References

American Association of Museums. (2006). *Museums working in the public interest.* Retrieved July 18, 2006, from http://www.aam-us.org/aboutmuseums/public interest.cfm

American Zoological Association. (2006). *Guide to accreditation of zoological parks and aquariums.* Retrieved August 17, 2006, from http://www.aza.org/Accreditation/ Documents/AccredGuide.pdf

Bell, S. (2003). Cyber-guest lecturers: Using Webcasts as a teaching tool. *Tech Trends, 47,* 10–14.

Burch, P., & Spillane, J. P. (2003). Elementary school leadership strategies and subject matter: Reforming mathematics and literacy instruction. *The Elementary School Journal, 103,* 519–535.

Chapin, J. R. (2005). *Elementary social studies: A practical guide.* Boston: Allyn & Bacon.

Consortium of National Arts Education. (1994). *National standards for arts education.* Reston, VA: Music Educators National Conference.

Cooper, D. (2003). A virtual dig: Joining archaeology and fiction to promote critical and historical thinking. *Social Studies, 94,* 69–73.

Covington, M. V. (1998). *The will to learn: A guide for motivating young people.* New York: Cambridge University Press.

Cox-Petersen, A., Marsh, D., Kisiel, J., & Melber, L. M. (2003). Investigation of guided school tours, student learning, and science reform recommendations at a museum of natural history. *Journal for Research in Science Teaching, 40,* 200–218.

Cox-Petersen, A., & Melber, L. M. (1999). Create a classroom museum. *Science Scope, 20,* 38–41.

Cox-Petersen, A. M., & Melber, L. M. (2001). Using technology to prepare and extend field trips. *The Clearing House, 75,* 18–20.

Croom L. (1997). Mathematics for all students: Access, excellence, and equity. In National Council of Teachers of Mathematics (Ed.), *Multicultural and gender equity in the mathematics classroom* (pp. 1–9). Reston, VA: National Council for the Teaching of Mathematics.

Csikszentmihalyi, M., & Hermanson, K. (1995). Intrinsic motivation in museums: Why does one want to learn? In J. H. Falk & L. D. Dierking (Eds.), *Public institutions for personal learning: Establishing a research agenda* (pp. 67–77). Washington, DC: American Association of Museums.

Dewey, J. (1938). *Experience and education.* New York: Macmillan.

Diket, R. M. (2003). The arts contribution to adolescent learning. *Kappa Delta Pi Record, 39,* 173–177.

Falk, J., & Dierking, L. (1997). School field trips: Assessing their long-term impact. *Curator, 40,* 211–218.

Falk, J. H., Martin, W. W., & Balling, J. D. (1978). The novel field trip phenomena: Adjustment to novel settings interferes with task learning. *Journal of Research in Science Teaching, 15,* 127–134.

Frey, B. B., Lee, S. W., Tollefson, N., Pass, L., & Massengill, D. (2005). Balanced literacy in an urban school district. *Journal of Educational Research, 98,* 272–280.

Gardner, H. (1991). *The unschooled mind: How children think and how schools should teach.* New York: Basic Books.

Greenes, C., Ginsburg, H. P., & Balfanz, R. (2004). Big math for little kids. *Early Childhood Research Quarterly, 19,* 159–166.

Griffin, J., & Symington, D. (1997). Moving from task-oriented to learning-oriented strategies on school excursions to museums. *Science Education, 81,* 763–779.

Guthrie, J. T., Wigfield, A., & Vonsecker, C. (2000). Effects of integrated instruction on motivation and strategy use in reading. *Journal of Educational Psychology, 92,* 331–341.

Harvey, S. (2002). Nonfiction inquiry: Using real reading and writing to explore the world. *Language Arts, 80*(1), 12–22.

Heward, W. L., & Orlansky, M. D. (1992). Exceptional children: An introductory survey of special education (4th ed.). New York: Maxwell Macmillan.

Hootstein, E. W. (1993). Motivational strategies and beliefs of U.S. history teachers at the middle school level. *Journal of Social Studies Research, 16*(2), 28–33.

Huinker, D. (1996). Teaching mathematics and science in urban elementary schools. *School Science and Mathematics, 96,* 340–349.

International Society for Educational Technology. (1998). *National education technology standards.* Retrieved August 17, 2006, from http://cnets.iste.org/students/s_stands.html

Kisiel, J. F. (2003). Teachers, museums and worksheets: A closer look at a learning experience. *Journal of Science Teacher Education, 14*(1), 3–21.

Klentschy, M. (2002). Helping English learners increase achievement through inquiry-based science instruction. *Bilingual Research Journal, 26,* 213–239.

Koff, S. R. (2000). Toward a definition of dance education. *Childhood Education, 77*(1), 27–31.

Korn, R. (2005). *Engaging our communities.* New Haven, CT: Peabody Museum of Natural History.

Ladson-Billings, G. (1995). Making mathematics meaningful in multicultural contexts. In W. G. Secada, E. Fennema, & L. B. Adajian (Eds.), *New directions for equity in mathematics education* (pp. 126–145). Cambridge, UK: Cambridge University Press.

Lapp, D., Fisher, D., & Flood, J. (1999). *Integrating the language arts and content areas: Effective research-based strategies.* (ERIC Document Reproduction Service No. ED 439 417)

MacCleod, F. (2004). Literacy identify and agency: Linking classrooms to communities. *Early Child Development and Care, 174,* 243–252.

Marcotte, S. (2006). Connect with tech! *Science Activities, 43,* 13–18.

Maslow, A. (1962). *Toward a psychology of being.* New York: VonNostrand.

Melber, L. M. (2003). *Maternal scaffolding strategies in two museum exhibition halls.* Unpublished doctoral dissertation, University of Southern California.

National Council for the Social Studies. (1993). Vision of powerful teaching and learning in the social studies: Building social understanding and civic efficacy (NCSS position statement). *Social Education, 57,* 213–223.

National Council for the Social Studies. (1994). *Curriculum standards for social studies: Expectations of excellence.* Washington, DC: National Council for the Social Studies.

National Council of Teachers of English & International Reading Association. (1996). *Standards for the English language arts.* Urbana, IL: National Council of Teachers of English.

National Council of Teachers of Mathematics. (1991). *Professional standards for teaching mathematics.* Reston, VA: National Council on the Teaching of Mathematics.

National Council of Teachers of Mathematics. (2000). *Principles and standards for school mathematics.* Reston, VA: National Council of Teachers.

National Research Council. (1996). *National science education standards.* Washington, DC: National Academy Press.

National Research Council. (1999). *How people learn: Brain, mind, experience, and school.* Washington, DC: National Academy Press.

National Science Resources Center, National Academy of Sciences, & Smithsonian Institution. (1997). *Science for all children: A guide to improving elementary science education in your district.* Washington, DC: National Academy Press.

National Science Teachers Association. (1998). An NSTA position statement: Informal science education. *Journal of College Science Teaching, 28,* 17–18.

Novick, R. (2000). Supporting early literacy development: Doing things with words in the real world. *Childhood Education, 76*(2), 70–75.

Pace, S., & Tesi, R. (2004). Adult's perception of field trips taken within grades K–12: Eight case studies in the New York metropolitan area. *Education, 125,* 30–40.

Price, S., & Hein, G. E. (1991). More than a field trip: Science programmes for elementary school groups at museums. *International Journal of Science Education, 13,* 505–519.

Reed, C. (1996). Projecting real world audiences. *The Writing Instructor, 15,* 131–139.

Roberts, L. C. (1997). *From knowledge to narrative: Educators and the changing museum.* Washington, DC: Smithsonian Institution Press.

Rosenthal, M. M., & Ampadu, C. K. (1999). Making mathematics real: The Boston math trail. *Mathematics Teaching in the Middles School, 5*(3), 140–147.

Ross, J. (2005). A hidden soul of artistry: Thinking in forgotten areas of the arts. *Phi Delta Kappan, 87*(1), 32–37.

Rule, A. C., & Barrera, M. T. (2003). Using objects to teach vocabulary words with more than one meaning. *Montessori LIFE, 15,* 14–17.

Seedfeldt, C. (2005). *Social studies for the preschool-primary child* (7th ed.). New York: Prentice Hall.

Serrell, B. (1996). *Exhibit labels: An interpretive approach.* Walnut Creek, CA: AltaMira.

Sheilds, P. (1998). Bringing history alive. *Canadian Social Studies, 32,* 65–66.

Smithsonian Institution. (2001). *Increasing museum visitation by under represented audiences: An exploratory study of art museum practices.* Washington, DC: Publication Office of Policy & Analysis, Smithsonian Institution.

Stohr-Hunt, P. (1996). An analysis of frequency of hands-on experience and science achievement. *Journal of Research in Science Teaching, 33,* 101–109.

Stronck, D. R. (1983). The comparative effects of different museum tours on children's attitudes and learning. *Journal of Research in Science Teaching, 20*(4), 283–290.

Taylor, S. I., Morris, V. G., & Cordeau-Young, C. (1997). Field trips in early childhood settings: Expanding the walls of the classroom. *Early Childhood Education Journal, 25,* 141–146.

Thornton, S. J. (1997). First-hand study: Teaching history for understanding. *Social Education, 61,* 11–12.

U.S. Department of Education. (2004). *A guide to education and "No Child Left Behind."* Washington, D.C.: Office of Public Affairs.

Watson, S. M. R., & Houtz, L. E. (2002). Teaching science: Meeting the academic needs of culturally and linguistically diverse students. *Intervention in School and Clinic, 37,* 267–278.

Weber-Russell, S., & LeBlanc, M. D. (2004). Learning by seeing by doing: Arithmetic word problems. *Journal of the Learning Sciences, 13,* 197–220.

Wenglinsky, H. (2000). *How teaching matters: Bringing the classroom back into discussions of teacher quality.* Report of the Policy Information Center, Educational Testing Service. (ERIC Document Reproduction Service No. ED 447 128).

Wise, K. (1996). Strategies for teaching science that works. *The Clearing House, 69,* 337–338.

Wolins, I. S., Jensen, N., & Ulzheimer, R. (1992). Children's memories of museum field trips: A qualitative study. *Journal of Museum Education, 17,* 17–27.

Index